THE
Manipulative
MAN

Identify His **Behavior,**
Counter the **Abuse,**
Regain **Control**

Dorothy McCoy, Ed.D.

Adams Media
Avon, Massachusetts

Published by Adams Media, a division of F+W Media, Inc.
57 Littlefield Street
Avon, MA 02322
www.adamsmedia.com

ISBN 10: 1-59337-623-5
ISBN 13: 973-1-59337-623-9
Printed in the United States of America.

10 9 8 7

Library of Congress Cataloging in Publication Data
McCoy, Dorothy.
The manipulative man / Dorothy McCoy.
p.   cm.
Includes bibliographical references.
ISBN 1-59337-623-5
1. Man-woman relationships—Psychological aspects. 2. Men—Psychology.
3. Manipulative behavior. 4. Typology (Psychology) 5. Personality disorders.
I. Title.
HQ801.M486 2006
646.7'70874—dc22
2006005006

This publication is designed to provide accurate and authoritative information with regard to the subject matter covered. It is sold with the understanding that the publisher is not engaged in rendering legal, accounting, or other professional advice. If legal advice or other expert assistance is required, the services of a competent professional person should be sought.

> —From a *Declaration of Principles* jointly adopted by a
> Committee of the American Bar Association and
> a Committee of Publishers and Associations

Many of the designations used by manufacturers and sellers to distinguish their products are claimed as trademarks. Where those designations appear in this book and Adams Media was aware of a trademark claim, the designations have been printed with initial capital letters.

This book is available at quantity discounts for bulk purchases.
For information, please call 1-800-289-0963.

Dedication

THIS BOOK IS dedicated to the men and women in blue who have given their lives while serving and protecting their communities.

There are more than 870,000 sworn law enforcement officers now serving in the United States, which is the highest figure ever. About 11.7 percent of those are female.

In 2004, there were more than 1.4 million violent crimes committed in the United States (according to the National Crime Victimization Survey conducted by the Bureau of Justice Statistics). The annual number of violent crimes has declined by 35 percent since it peaked in 1993 at 4 million.

Crime fighting has taken its toll. Since the first recorded police death in 1792, there have been more than 17,000 law enforcement officers killed in the line of duty. Currently, there are 17,081 names engraved on the walls of the National Law Enforcement Officers Memorial.

A total of 1,649 law enforcement officers died in the line of duty during the past ten years, an average of one death every 53.5 hours or 164 per year. There were 153 law enforcement officers killed in 2004.—Data from the National Law Enforcement Officer Memorial Fund (*www.nleomf.com/TheMemorial/Facts*)

Contents

Acknowledgments

THIS HAS BEEN an especially hectic and challenging year. Friends, family, and professional associates have been particularly important in helping me survive the last several months. Finishing this book and another book (competing for my time and attention) has necessitated a big, chunky chain effectively thwarting my escape attempts. Warm thanks go to Sophie, the world-class snorer, for dutifully sharing my detention. Each thoughtful gesture, loving thought, and/or expression of support was especially endearing during my period of imprisonment.

Many heartfelt thanks to my dear friends Deputy Gary Goss, S.C. Criminal Justice Instructor Sandy Caudill, Pepper Sarnoff, Captain Keith Rogers, and, of course, my wise agent Nancy Rosenfeld. You were there for me, checking on me, insisting I remember to eat, and showing your love in various and sundry ways.

A special salute and "I love you" goes to Sergeant Keith Alan Crosby. I assure you, Keith; every kindness was greatly appreciated and duly noted. To my beloved, Cyndi Carpenter, what can I say? You have been a blessing every day of your life (well, most days . . .). I cannot imagine my life without Ginny de Freitas. She unfailingly supports me in my spells of incredible stupidity, my occasional triumphs, and my unpredictable pursuits. I am ridiculously proud of each of you.

It is difficult to contain my emotions when I think of my benevolent editors. Paula Munier and Andrea Norville, you have consistently inspired me with your gentle counsel ("Writers don't need sleep . . . drink more coffee!"). Words to live by . . . .

CHAPTER 1

Manipulation,
Thy Name Is Man

Don't you think that any secret course is an unworthy one?
⇜ Charles Dickens

WOMEN ARE MESMERIZED by the forbidden relationship, the exciting stranger who radiates danger and yet seems vulnerable and wounded by life. We want to crush him to our breasts and ease his pain. Simultaneously, we desire the thrill and the exhilarating sting of danger. We want to be *the* one woman who by virtue of her unconditional love will transform him into the perfect lover. Yes, we are certain we will succeed where lesser women have failed.

Women also adore the "little boy" who has never quite managed to grow up. He simply needs the love of a good woman to blossom into Indiana Jones. He needs love, approval, and acceptance from us to achieve the self-confidence he has been denied. We see a wonderful, sweet man, full of promise and potential, waiting for someone to believe in him as only we can.

These are a couple of the myths we embrace over and over again. The manipulators perpetuate these myths (and others), and, oh, they have many, many brothers. You will meet the brotherhood of manipulative men in this book. There is the too-good-to-be-true stranger who will steal your Corvette and max out your credit cards. The feckless boy-man who will allow you to be his mom, assume responsibility for his actions, or the lack thereof, and grant each of his whims.

I bet you have met one of the manipulators. Did he promise you the stars and play you like a musical instrument? Many women have fallen for the illusion because it is so expertly conceived and performed. Nevertheless, please don't worry, you are not unintelligent or gullible, much of their irresistible attraction is chemical. Another stumbling stone is our nurturing nature (which is culturally encouraged). Fortunately, you do have the power to change your beliefs and behaviors and become less susceptible.

Have no fear, you can learn to recognize a manipulator, avoid their traps, and live as the incredible woman you are, not the woman they choose to create. Stay with me, and we will explore the top nine "least-wanted list" of manipulative types in order to avoid them, housetrain them (if they are willing), and/or learn to outmaneuver them. Tighten your seat belt; this will be an incredible ride.

Do you have a man in your life who doesn't play by the rules? Unfortunately, manipulation as a tool for achieving one's goals is not rare, nor is it a modern adaptation. Remember the biblical story about Joseph and his coat of many colors? Joseph was manipulated by his envious brothers. Charles Manson manipulated naive young girls; Stalin and Hitler manipulated entire nations. We all use manipulation to some extent, but some individuals depend on it to feed their egos and reach their narcissistic goals. Manipulative behavior is used to influence and control others for one's own benefit. Normally, manipulative behavior is covert, because if we recognize it we would don a garlic necklace and learn to protect ourselves. That is the purpose of this book: a garlic necklace, silver bullet, and wolfsbane to protect you from the manipulators who would selfishly use you.

Manipulation, thy name is Man. We often hear that women manipulate to create a level playing field because men are larger and more physically powerful. Perhaps this is true. However, men are experts at manipulative behaviors and play it as if it were Saturday afternoon football. Well, they have scored enough points. If you know how to counter manipulation, you can strengthen your relationships; intimacy does not grow in an inequitable environment. You can make free choices based on your beliefs and experiences, and in your best interest. At times, it is in your best interest to leave a manipulative relationship when it cannot be changed or it is inherently unhealthy. Take heart, frequently the casual manipulator will, with guidance, "see the light," adapt his behavior, and work with you to create a mutually gratifying, loving relationship.

Why do men manipulate? There are many reasons and none of them are justifiable. Here are some of the more obvious and common reasons:

- To get their own way
- To prevent you from making a free choice
- To feel in control and powerful
- To impose their reality on you
- To avoid responsibility
- To gain an unfair advantage
- To distort reality
- To preserve their distorted self-concept
- To diminish you
- To discourage intimacy
- To coerce

These goals are only examples; sometimes a man may manipulate simply from habit. Habits become ingrained; manipulators reach for the familiar tool rather than exploring the situation and choosing the most effective tool. In "Habit," Chapter IV in his *Principles of Psychology*, William James (1890–1981) made one of modern psychology's first pronouncements on the course of adult development:

> *Already at the age of twenty-five you see the professional mannerism settling down on the young commercial traveler, on the young doctor, on the young minister, on the young counselor-at-law. You see the little lines of cleavage running through the character, the tricks of thought, the prejudices, the ways of the "shop," in a word, from which the man can by-and-by no more escape than his coat sleeve can suddenly fall into a new set of folds . . . In most of us, by the age of thirty, the character has set like plaster, and will never soften again.* (pp. 125–126)

Fortunately, that is not quite true, but for the person with a personality disorder or severe maladaptive personality traits (without fully meeting the criteria for a personality disorder) substantial change is unlikely.

Who Manipulates?

Individuals with personality disorders frequently employ manipulative behaviors. Others may also focus on achieving their goals at any cost. Nonetheless, they probably have characteristics in common with individuals who meet the criteria in the *DSM-IV-TR* (a manual of the American Psychiatric Association) for a personality disorder. Their cloaked influence may be subtle or obvious, but you can depend on one thing: they will deny using manipulation or they will reframe it in a positive way. As Dr. Harriet Braiker, author of *Who's Pulling Your Strings,* says, "The reason manipulation persists is because . . . it works. And the counter-control that a victim has, is to make it stop working." Therefore, your power is in your ability to see beneath the manipulator's words into his scheming thinking process. You would be surprised how easy it becomes with a little practice. Once you understand his true purpose, his manipulative behavior loses its power to influence you.

We are accustomed to some forms of subtle manipulation. For example, salespersons, news commentators, and politicians are often suspected of being less-than-completely trustworthy. Unless one is extremely naive, one knows to throw in a grain of salt when interpreting their messages. Again, they have an agenda and their goals may not be our goals. However, when manipulation occurs in an intimate relationship, a personal trust has been broken and someone we love and trust has taken advantage of us.

Manipulators have many faces. Fortunately, you can learn to recognize them. This may help.

Let's Meet the Personality Disorders

Manipulators consider a relationship either a contest of wits, which they play exceptionally well, or a way in which to have their needs met. Could you learn to manipulate and beat them at their own game? Don't even think it; they will win. They are experts and you are an amateur. There is a price to pay when a person habitually manipulates, and that price is distance and isolation. Intimacy is only a vague concept to the manipulative man or woman.

Author of *How to Spot Dangerous Men Before You Get Involved,* counselor Sandra Brown warns that men with ingrained personality disorders are incapable of making healthy adaptive changes, no matter how sincere they may sound. Some men cannot change, and others have no interest in changing. They will attempt to manipulate your emotions to keep you in an inequitable relationship. You will notice self-serving behaviors (i.e., forgetting his wallet at restaurants; not calling when he will be late) very early in the relationship if you pay close attention to what they do, *not what they say.*

Knowledge is power. So, let's learn more about personality disorders and the traits that make individuals qualify for the diagnosis (he may have some of the traits but does not meet the criteria for a specific personality disorder), what makes them tick, and how to recognize their manipulative behaviors. All of the manipulative men in this book have one or more of the personality disorder characteristics listed here.

Personality Disorders and Characteristics

Antisocial
Beginning early in life, these antisocial individuals display a talent for getting into trouble. Many end up in conflict with the law and are incarcerated. They can be charming and fun; but it is a bumpy ride, and you pay for the gas. They are remorseless and impulsive. If you want to have fun, they will show you a good time. When it is time to be a responsible adult, however, they won't be around. Their goal is to have fun and live dangerously.
Common Manipulation: He will find your vulnerability and use it to control you.

Borderline
Borderline individuals are highly emotional and tend to idealize relationships and then vilify them. They are on an

emotional roller coaster, and they will take friends and family along for the ride. They are fearful of abandonment and will display extreme behavior if you leave the relationship. In *DSM Made Easy*, Dr. James Morrison says of people with borderline personality disorders, "They are uncertain about who they are, and lack the ability to maintain stable interpersonal relationships."

Common Manipulation: He will threaten to harm himself to keep you in the relationship.

Histrionic

These individuals can be sexually seductive and overly emotional, and they seek attention. They are willing to do whatever it takes to remain on center stage. Early in a relationship, they can be fun and interesting. Soon, however, one discovers that they do not have strong feeling about anything that does not pertain to them and their desire for attention. They are vain and invest heavily in their appearance.

Common Manipulation: He will seduce you into meeting his need for constant attention.

Narcissistic

These men see themselves as the center of the universe. If you wish to have a relationship with one of them (and why would you?), you had better agree with him. They do not take constructive criticism well. They want to be pampered and admired; nothing else will meet their demanding expectations.

Common Manipulation: He will pursue and win you with calculated too-good-to-be-true pseudo-charm, and then he will drain you dry.

Dependent

Dependent men desperately need the approval of others and fear making independent decisions. They will cling to a relationship to avoid being alone. They require a great deal of affirmation and reassurance. The end of a relationship is a crisis for them and they will attempt to hold on. They may become quite emotional.

Common Manipulation: These men are just so darn nice and are certainly willing to do anything to avoid conflict or abandonment. Wait, this niceness comes with an overwhelming dependency.

Psychopath

Successful psychopaths (believe me, they are not all in jail) can charm you out of your heart, your knickers, and your trust fund before you know what is happening. Even when they disappear without a word, you may still staunchly defend them. It is their talent. Listen to your instinct on this one; warning flags featuring a skull and crossbones will flap vigorously in their wake. I was told by a police officer that the hair on the back of his neck stands up when he meets a psychopath. I hope you are so lucky.

Common Manipulation: Much like the narcissistic manipulator (and he may be both), the psychopath can be sinfully, stunningly charming, frequently highly intelligent, and again, too good to be true. When you fall for the attractive package, be aware it comes equipped with incredibly shallow emotions and a staggering price tag. If you want empathy and love—pick another model.

Most men you meet will probably not qualify for a formal personality disorder diagnosis. However, they may have a number of the characteristics described in the *DSM-IV-TR* criteria.

Personality-disordered persons are probably no more than 10 percent of the general population (this varies from study to study). You may know a number of men who have some, or even many, of the characteristics. Individuals with personality disorders (or traits) commonly use manipulation to achieve their goals.

Also, according to the *ICD-10*, the mental health manual used in Europe, the following characteristics are associated with personality disorders:

- Callous unconcern for the feelings of others
- Gross and persistent attitude of irresponsibility and disregard for social norms, rules, and obligations
- Incapacity to maintain enduring relationships, though having no difficulty in establishing them
- Very low tolerance to frustration and a low threshold for discharge of aggression, including violence
- Incapacity to experience guilt or to profit from experience, particularly punishment
- Marked proneness to blame others, or to offer plausible rationalizations, for the behavior that has brought the patient into conflict with society

Callous unconcern can be mistaken for manly reticence. You may think that he controls his emotions well. A John Wayne—the strong, silent type with a heart of gold. Be careful, he may not have a heart.

The *irresponsible* man may appear to be fun, a free spirit, like a Corvette. Keep in mind, Corvettes use the highest priced fuel, have little space for luggage, and frequently leak. A less glamorous SUV might be more practical and less costly in the long run.

You may believe that a man who is *incapable of maintaining an enduring relationship* is tragically poetic. You would be mistaken. If his relationships are to endure over time, a man must be able to connect emotionally with a woman, strive to understand her needs, and attempt to meet those needs. Many disordered men and many maladjusted men (they have some of the character traits but do not meet the criteria for a diagnosis) do not have the skills and/or the desire to maintain an intimate, caring relationship.

Women sometimes mistakenly believe that a man with a *low level of tolerance to frustration and the discharge of aggression* is an exciting, hat-bearing Indiana Jones. Actually, low frustration means reacting aggressively in situations in which other men might feel mildly irked, if they have any reaction. In the article "Frustration-Aggression Reformulation," Berkowitz (1989) discussed the association between frustration, expectations and aggression: "An unanticipated failure to obtain an attractive goal is more unpleasant than an expected failure, and it is the greater displeasure in the former case that gives rise to the stronger instigation to aggression. . . . the thwarted person's appraisals and attributions presumably determine how bad they feel." Psychopaths, antisocial individuals, and narcissists and their wannabes fully believe they "should" reach their goals no matter how unreasonable or ridiculous their expectations might be. These men have immense egos and do not react reasonably if they are thwarted or frustrated. You cannot "win" in such a relationship. Attempting to predict how he will respond, even in perfectly innocuous situations, is fraught with danger.

A man who exhibits *incapacity to experience guilt or to profit from experience, particularly punishment,* is a bad little boy who will never grow up. If this is what you are looking for, this is your "man." You must understand, however, that saying something such as "It frightens me when you do that" will have absolutely no effect on him. In addition, he may have lost jobs, made enemies, and damaged relationships because he cannot govern his temper or keep his promises. Having those undesirable experiences will probably not stimulate him to alter his behavior.

The man who exhibits a *marked proneness to blame others, or to offer plausible rationalizations,* will tell you, and you may choose to believe him, that he is maltreated by the world. What compassionate woman would not feel a yearning to champion a man so unjustly wronged? Unfortunately, after a short time, he will decide that you, too, are one of the malfeasants who mistreat him. Be assured, if he did "it," he will manufacture a perfectly plausible explanation for doing "it."

The Dark Side

Some traits and behaviors are beneficial and adaptive unless they are carried to extremes. For example, when looking at the following two lists, notice that the first list contains traits that are either positive or neutral. The second list contains extremes of each trait. They are no longer neutral, harmless, endearing, or positive. Remember, human beings are purposeful. If he has extreme personality traits, there is probably a payoff or he would have stopped using the behaviors that are associated with that trait.

Once you understand his goal (the payoff), you will understand your role in his life, if you should decide to accept the role. For example, if he is arrogant (i.e., narcissistic, psychopathic), he "needs" continuous adoration, and he will use whatever manipulative techniques he deems necessary to achieve his goal. That, by the way, would be your role in his life.

Neutral or Positive	Dark Side	His Goal
Nurturing	Smothering	To control you
Confident	Arrogant	Adoration
Offbeat personality	Quirky	To be alone
Intense interest	Jealous and possessive	Protect fragile ego
Spontaneous	Irresponsible	To be taken care of
Strong-willed, persistent	Stubborn, inflexible	Total compliance
Shy	Timid	To be protected
Sensual and sexual	Promiscuous	To win a sexual trophy
Relaxed	Muddled	Mothering
Successful	Workaholic	To avoid intimacy
Flattering	Superficial	Shallow relationships
Sense of humor	Silly	An audience
Sweet and sensitive	Thin-skinned	Endless affirmation

Adapted from Spitzberg and Cupach, 1998, page 13.

It is sometimes difficult to recognize the difference between a virtue and a trait that has gone to the dark side. If you are not sure, you probably need to collect additional data. Ask yourself if the trait or behavior leads to intimacy. Does it create distance? Do you feel controlled? Do you feel overwhelmed or used? Do you feel confused? Do you feel as if you are going crazy? These are clues that something is amiss and you might want to take a closer, more objective look at the man and his behavior.

A Gentler Theory of Personality

Some mental health professionals believe that the personality disorders and their exacting criteria are not an appropriate way to categorize pathology in individuals. Others dare to question the concept of pathology altogether. They wonder if we are in fact creating pathology by labeling individuals. They question if personality traits define what we perceive and how we perceive it. This new concept suggests using a variety of factors; it allows us to consider all of the applicable influences (i.e., society, genetics) on who we are as emotional, cognitive beings. Mary Murphy, in *Psychology Today*, explicates this "new" perspective on personality, " . . . the new view of personality heralds a revolution in how we view disorder, marking a shift away from rigid categories of pathology . . . to the way individuals fit in their world." In other words, we may fit comfortably into our unique niche because of a personality quirk. Obsessive-Compulsive Personality Disorder could be exceptionally beneficial to an individual in some careers. For example, Einstein used his extraordinary intelligence and ability to focus on minute details to explore time and distance and how we understand our world (two observers who move relative to each other will measure different time and space intervals for the same events).

Therefore, as we discuss the diverse personality types in the following chapters, let's remember we are focusing on a limited number of characteristics as they pertain to relationships. Our primary focus is manipulation and understanding how various personalities use it to gain an advantage or reach a goal. Categories are generalizations that are relatively accurate when used to make assumptions and predict outcomes for a large number of individuals.

I will admit that ferreting out someone's goals based on their personality traits and behaviors takes patience and practice. However, once you understand a man's goals, you can determine if you really desire a relationship with him. Again, knowledge is power. Why don't we turn to the next chapter and explore the Mama's Boy.

He may at first glance appear genuinely thoughtful; after all, he loves his mother. As you know, appearances can be deceiving. I'll bet we will understand his goals before the end of the chapter.

CHAPTER 2

The
Mama's Boy

Men say they love independence in a woman, but they don't waste a second demolishing it brick by brick.
↩ *Candice Bergen*

A MAMA'S BOY may be unusually attached to his mother—or not. A man may be considered a Mama's Boy because he has characteristics normally associated with women. Joseph Malinak (2005) defines Mama's Boy as " . . . a man who has not been grounded in the masculine field." Let's give them their due: they are cute, cuddly, and frequently agreeable. Mama's Boys are the teddy bears of the manipulators. They have learned how to please women. Their goal is to ensure feminine approval (usually Mama's) and thereby the rewards that accompany such approval.

As their name implies, "Mother" will always come first, even when she is only a venerable memory. In the stereotypical Mama's Boy–Mama relationship, their devotion to "Mother" isn't simply the love and admiration that most of us feel for our mothers. It is more palpable than the deference to parents that is esteemed in our culture. Their "good son" behaviors are excessive, sometimes bordering on an obsession.

The Mama's Boy is in a symbiotic relationship with his mother. Both are receiving something of supreme importance to them from their connection. This means, if you plan to make a few nips and tucks in the way the mother and the son relate to each other, you will probably discover they are quite resistant. In this parent-offspring drama, the mother is usually the stronger character. However, your Mama's Boy will also cling tenaciously to his predominant relationship. Fear not, there is good news. Human beings are supremely capable of being both flexible and adaptive. In fact, we would not have survived as a species otherwise, and he is a human being.

Perhaps we can look to the father of modern psychology for psychoanalysis of the Mama's Boy. Interestingly, Dr. Freud was very close to his mother and acknowledged "considerable hostility" toward his father (Bland, 1998). In his Oedipus complex, Freud attempts to explain the process by which we become culturally accepted members of our gender. According to his theory, boys cling to their mothers, their most powerful influence, until they are about four years old. Mother has been the one who most intimately knows her son. She has bathed, nursed, and protected him. He has probably seen her unclothed. Then a gender crisis occurs, and he feels compelled by his father and other males to reject his mother and emulate his father.

What if the male gender crisis never occurs? What if he continues to seek power through the person who, until age four, was seemingly all-powerful? Culture and gender exert great pressure to force males to reject the feminine and become "one of the boys." What if a male resists this pressure? His identity may stay rooted to his mother-son relationship and how this interaction influences his other male-female relationships.

Therefore, if their mother is all-powerful, Mama's Boys long for her to make their decisions or at least continuously to reassure them. They may be frightened of making ordinary human mistakes because maternal disapproval may follow. Mama's Boys believe it is better to do nothing than take a risk. It is important to realize that although the mother-son dyad may be very close, it may conceal a love/hate relationship. These dynamics will likely flow over into other relationships with women.

Who will accept the overwhelming responsibility for these men who have never grown up? We do, my friends. We graciously shield them from a judgmental world, take the sting out of their interactions with society, and pet and defend them. After a while, we are shocked to realize that we have assumed an eternal obligation and the light at the end of the tunnel is a freight train. Then we panic. If we decide it would be rewarding actually to have a life, changes must be made. I sincerely doubt that Mama's Boy will be leading the charge.

Adjectives frequently associated with Mama's Boys include *indecisive, emotionally dependent, unreliable, whiny,* and *manipulative.* We are only human, and after a while *whiny* alone is enough to drive us to drink.

Perhaps you know a Mama's Boy? I think we have all dated one. Relating to and effectively communicating with him can be frustrating and maddening.

We can be ambivalent about our attraction to a Mama's Boy. In addition, if we decide to pursue a relationship with him, we must learn to cope effectively with his more bothersome behaviors—such as manipulation. Mama's Boys by definition have some behaviors and attitudes that are similar to criteria symptoms for Avoidant Personality Disorder and/or Dependent Personality Disorder. Also, he may throw in some narcissistic tendencies just to push you over the edge. The number and severity of "symptoms" will determine if your relationship is a mere nuisance or a catastrophe.

The Lost Mother: The Ideal Mother

You may be surprised to hear that a Mama's Boy may not have a mother. I have heard women say, "Well, I won't have to worry about a mother-in-law problem. His mother died years ago." Not so fast, sons who lose their mothers early bestow on them attributes that are cultural stereotypes about the perfect mom: unconditionally loving and all-nurturing. Children often idealize lost or missing parents. A son growing up without his mother can create a mother and then worship her. No flesh-and-blood woman can possibly live up to his romanticized vision of this perfect woman.

Cognitive, social, and emotional growth takes place at each stage of life. We cannot skip stages. Many adults who lost their mothers as children feel that they lost their childhood. It is possible that this tragedy can contribute to arrested development. Emotionally, children can remain stuck at the immature stage they were in when their mother died. Conversely, if other younger siblings must be cared for, the elder child may become an adult much too early. This could influence a child's sense of responsibility and create an overly responsible, high-achieving adult who may be fearful of loss. Also, losing a parent during childhood can influence coping behaviors that lead to lifelong depression.

Before you confidently announce that the motherless man cannot be a Mama's Boy, take the test and see if he meets the criteria. In fact, he will be the only man with a mother who is a blend of Betty Crocker, Mother Teresa, and Britney Spears. A few weeks of trying to live up to his extraordinary mom may change your mind. Depending on the circumstances under which he grew up, he could fit comfortably into either type: Clinging Mama's Boy or Spoiled Mama's Boy.

This is not to say that losing his mother dooms him to be forever emotionally unhealthy. Many variables contribute to personality, resilience, and mood development. The circumstances of her death, his genetic inheritance, and the availability of other nurturers are very important factors. Nonetheless, dear reader, I suggest that you proceed with due caution. In my experience, there are two distinct species of Mama's Boys. The first is the Spoiled Mama's Boy, who has been pampered all of his life. He is quite confident that he is entitled to ceaseless coddling. The other type is the Clinging Mama's Boy, who is hypersensitive and may feel inadequate. The shared commonality is a need for mothering by Mom or by anyone else willing to accept the responsibility.

Criteria for the Mama's Boy

Though the following behaviors, beliefs, and traits are characteristic of each type, it is highly unlikely one person will have them all.

How will you recognize a Mama's Boy? Look for the red flags. They will be there.

Spoiled Mama's Boy
- Preoccupied with himself
- Irresponsible
- Need for admiration
- Sense of entitlement
- Easily bruised ego
- Lack of understanding or concern for others

- A history of parental adoration
- Manipulative behavior to ensure that he receives the special attention he firmly believes is due to him

Clinging Mama's Boy
- Indecisive
- Fearful of criticism
- Desperate need for support and nurturing
- Fear of abandonment
- Helplessness
- Excessive need for reassurance
- Low self-esteem
- Depressed mood
- Manipulative behavior to ensure that he receives the nurturing he believes is essential to his survival

If your man has three or more of the traits for either category, plus the last behavior, then you can say with supreme confidence, "He may be a Mama's Boy." Most of the symptoms are open to interpretation. Therefore, you will have indicators rather than concrete facts.

Let's peek in on Janice and her Spoiled Mama's Boy (SMB), Larson.

Case Study #1: Larson and Janice

Janice, a busy attorney, dashes home after work each day to have dinner ready when SMB Larson finally arrives. Larson, a stockbroker with a spotty employment history, has been looking for gainful employment for several months. The poor SMB frantically searches for several hours every day. Exhausted by his harried efforts, he laments, "It is a jungle out there." A shadowy question lurks deep within Janice, but she ignores it whenever it creeps to the surface. Is it possible that Larson isn't spending all those hours looking for work?

Larson and his mother bewail the dearth of job opportunities appropriate for his exceptional ability and expertise. He resigned (in a huff) from previous positions because he was "unappreciated." These unfortunate financial inconveniences were never Larson's fault—according to Larson and Mom. He has the "woe is me" blue funks because no one, except dear old Madre, truly understands him.

Nonetheless, former coworkers have implied that he is arrogant, self-serving, and irresponsible and doesn't play well with others.

According to the Larson-and-Mom team, his increasingly severe financial problems are Janice's fault. If she would wise up, stop being a "do-gooder," and choose more lucrative cases, everything would be sunshine and roses. Janice is overwhelmed with financial concerns and feels guilty about doubting Larson. After all, didn't he tell her that he would find an employer worthy of him soon? "Trust me," he says.

Larson manipulated Janice using the following techniques:

LARSON'S MANIPULATIVE TECHNIQUES

Ganging up: Since Larson and his mother agreed on certain "fairly tales," their greater number made it appear that they were right.

Blaming: "It" can't be Larson's fault, because it is Janice's fault. "It" is also the fault of former employers and coworkers.

Manipulating the truth: Of course, Larson is frantically looking for a job. Yeah, right . . . .

Exaggeration: He is so talented and unique that he cannot find a job worthy of him.

Exploiting emotions: He uses Janice's tendency to feel guilty against her. He also uses Janice's sympathy for his enthusiastic, yet fruitless efforts to find employment. Manipulators will zero in on your vulnerability very quickly and effectively.

Let's listen in on another manipulator and notice how he wields unfair tactics to avoid responsibility.

Sample Dialogue for James and Michelle

Michelle is a twenty-eight-year-old personal assistant to a popular writer. Her hours are long, interesting, and filled with demanding tasks. She has been married for six years to James, the Chameleon. James has worked in ten different jobs since Michelle has known him. At first, she thought he had exceptionally poor luck in choosing employers. Then she began to wonder if he was as ineffectual at work as he was at home. The pattern became depressingly predictable. James does well on a new job for a few weeks and then becomes fretful and despondent and misses work. Soon, the inevitable blade falls and the company dismisses him.

Michelle is deeply concerned about their future, but she tries to be supportive. However, James dismisses her encouragement and mopes. Michelle clings tenaciously to her job for financial security. She works until after 6 P.M., so on most days, she needs James's help with their young son, Jimmie.

This is a recent telephone conversation.

MICHELLE: James, how did the meeting go with Jimmie's teacher? The meeting was scheduled for ten, wasn't it?

JAMES: Michelle, you know I feel uncomfortable talking to his teachers. Besides, I don't remember saying that I would go. Weren't you supposed to talk to her?

MICHELLE: No! We discussed this last night and you promised to take care of it. I am overloaded with work today. I was depending on you.

JAMES: Well, I forgot. You forget things sometimes too. You will just have to call her and explain. You always blame me; he is your child too. I have to go now.

MICHELLE: Okay, I will call her.

James used the following manipulative techniques to con Michelle:

Passive aggressive: "I forgot . . ."

Manipulating the truth: "I don't remember saying that I would go."

Blaming: "You always blame me. Weren't you supposed to talk to her?" (This could also fall under exploiting emotions—guilt.)

Whining: "You know I feel uncomfortable meeting with teachers."

See, you should have taken responsibility: "You will just have to call her and explain." This implies, "If you had taken care of this in the beginning, we wouldn't have a problem. Now would we?"

The list of possible manipulations is long and frustrating. These are a few of the more popular techniques. You may be able to identify these or others in your relationship. You probably noticed that James' manipulative tactics worked for him. This "win" will encourage him to continue avoiding responsibility and shifting it to Michelle.

Case Study #2: John and Anita

Anita called to make an appointment for couple's counseling. She said she had tried everything she could imagine to save her marriage. She read self-help books, talked to friends, talked to her husband, and watched marriage counseling on television. She was frantic; she had reached the end of her rope and didn't know what else to do. She hoped a professional would find the magic words to persuade her husband, John, to hear her before it was too late.

John was a large man, massive in both height and weight. He taught high school and coached. Anita was a petite, bespectacled blonde librarian. They had been married for three years and had a sixteen-month-old son, Kyle.

Anita was the first to speak. She was chomping at the bit to tell me about John's mother. Anita said that their marriage would be just fine if his mother would stop interfering. Anita was at her wit's end and didn't know what to do. Her words started to jumble together as her agitation increased. John jumped in to say (loudly) that his mother was only trying to help them and he found Anita's attitude extremely unappreciative. Anita countered that John always took his mother's side.

It was the second marriage for both. Anita had been attracted to John because he was "fun, sweet, and exciting." He was attracted to her because she seemed "dependable and nurturing."

Anita said their dating period was wonderful, until (*shiver*) she met Mom. According to Anita, Mom was unenthusiastic, aloof, and probably rode a broom to work everyday.

John called his mom daily and ate dinner with her a couple of times a week—without Anita. His dad had died when John was young and his mom had focused all of her affection on her only son. John grew up believing that he was entitled to pampering and special treatment not normally bestowed on the masses. That had been his childhood experience. Regrettably, for John, his first wife and various and sundry employers had vigorously disagreed.

I always ask clients how committed they are to their relationship on a scale of one to ten. One means that "I have my bags packed and I am waiting for an excuse." Ten means that "I would do anything within reason to save my marriage." I was pleased to hear that they were equally committed to their marriage. The homework assignment was to develop a unique vision of their ideal marriage. Together, they constructed their vision of "a nurturing, loving, trusting environment in which they could grow as individuals and as a couple." It was also agreed that they would equally share the responsibility for reaching this goal.

A couple's relationship goals are seldom a topic of discussion. Unfortunately, behaviors cannot be tied to goals that have never been verbalized. Now that their goals were explicit, we could work on the behaviors that were inconsistent with their vision. John realized that championing his mom did not lead to a more loving relationship with Anita. As we explored their families of origin, we discovered that Anita was the eldest of four children. She had learned a caretaking role very early in her life. John had learned a care-receiving role. They were made for each other.

Keep in mind that there were two people maintaining the inequitable balance in this relationship. John expected pampering and Anita provided it without asking for reciprocation. She started asking for what she wanted and needed and learned to say no if John was unfairly demanding or "forgot" to give as well as take. To John's surprise, Anita decided that being on the receiving end of nurturing might be an exceptionally pleasant experience.

John had a choice to make. He chose Anita and his young son. Mom learned that John would not come to dinner unless Anita was invited too. Mom was now also expected to be warm and fuzzy toward Anita—or John wouldn't visit. Anita and Mom actually began to tentatively appreciate each other— after all, they loved the same guy. Don't you just adore happy endings?

John's Manipulative Techniques

Blaming: Everything was Anita's fault. If she would just shape up, all would be well.

"Me"-centered arrogance: His message was "I should get what I want." What he wanted was his intact relationship with Mom and to be indulged by Anita.

Case Study #3: Ben and Lorie

Ben and Lorie had been dating for several months. Their early courtship was filled with superlatives—*wonderful, exciting, exhilarating,* and *absolutely marvelous.* Ben was generous with his compliments, and Lorie felt beautiful and desirable. After a few weeks, however, the course of their new relationship veered off in an entirely new direction—emotional, argumentative, and critical. Lorie felt shock and disbelief. Where had the enchanting man she met gone? From where had Mr. Egotistical come? However, she was optimistic they could regain that initial thrill.

On the six-month anniversary of their first date, Ben stopped calling. She called his cell phone and office to no avail. She left messages. He did not return her calls. After a few days, she began to get the message. Mr. Wonderful/Egotistical had moved on to greener pastures. Those greener pastures included an uninformed woman who would unconditionally adore him (for a while). Lorie had not had the privilege of meeting Ben's mother and sisters or she would have known that Ben had unrealistic relationship expectations and why.

Once Ben knew that Lorie expected a reciprocal relationship, he could no longer maintain his false self—the perfect little boy Ben. He had learned from his mother and three adoring sisters that he was special and should not have to work at relationships. He needed the false self-image of a little boy who should be petted and adored more than he needed Lorie; so, he moved on without a backward glance.

BEN'S MANIPULATIVE TECHNIQUES

Charm: Most egocentric Mama's Boys appeal to us because they can be attractive, well educated, verbally fluent, well mannered, attentive, and appearance conscious. They use these well-tended personal qualities to persuade women to admire them.

Insincere flattery: Ben peered into Lorie's self-doubts and flattered those areas. This is not to say that every man who flatters you is insincere. Watch for an enduring pattern and consistency; as always, the truth is consistent. Insincere compliments dry up in the blink of an eye.

It is a good idea to watch your beloved interact with his family. These interactions will give you clues about what he expects from you and how you will be treated.

Starring the Mama's Boy

Elvis Presley was certainly the most famous, talented, and gorgeous Mama's Boy. An early photo of Elvis, singing to hot-and-bothered fans, taken by his friend Roger Marshutz shows Elvis wearing a velvet shirt his mother made for him. Elvis was eighteen when he walked into a Memphis studio and paid $4 to record "My Happiness" and "That's When Your Heartaches Begin" as a present for his mother. Elvis loved his mother and referred to her as his "baby." Because of her melancholy moods, their roles were reversed at times and the child became the parent.

We are all aware of his excesses. Are they related to his devoted relationship with his dependent, yet doting mother? The only two people who know are no longer able to speak for themselves, unless you have a functional Ouija board. I attempt to avoid making psychological deductions about individuals unless we have at least spoken. That said, it appears that the unprecedented adoration of millions of fans couldn't replace Elvis' loss when his mom died in 1958. Whenever I think of Elvis and his mother, I feel sad. I would like to believe that they are together now; singing the venerable old hymns they loved.

Classic Mama's Boy Elvis may have expected more attention from his wife and girlfriends than the average man does. Also, he may have taken less responsibility for his relationships because he was accustomed to adoration. Since every woman under sixty-five on this clay and granite planet also worshiped him, his sense of entitlement may have expanded.

Dealing with a Mama's Boy

The Rules: Write Them

Your boundaries should be very clear. In other words, your MB must know what behaviors are acceptable and which ones will ignite a swift response. Be very clear about this. If you expect him to accept half of the responsibilities in the relationship, then you need to say so. Writing a contract of responsible behaviors (he can contribute to this too—sorry) is very prudent. Your contract might look something like John and Anita's contract:

Our Contract of Shared Responsibilities

Anita's Responsibilities	John's Responsibilities
Take care of the cat	Take care of the dogs
Cook Monday, Wednesday, and Friday	Cook Tuesday and Thursday
Wash dishes when John cooks	Wash dishes when Anita cooks
Fix coffee in the morning on odd days	Fix coffee on even days
I take care of my car	He takes care of his car
I buy needed groceries on even days	He buys on odd days
We pool our money after taking out 20 percent (fun money)	Each will spend his/her fun money as he or she sees fit.
Visit my parents once a week	He visits his once a week
Bathe and read to child on odd days	Bathe and read to child on even days

Whatever you include in the contract should be as specific and inclusive as possible to avoid misunderstandings or passive-aggressive reactions (i.e., I forgot, you never said . . .). If both agree, the contract can be changed at any time. Be flexible, but keep the flexibility within reasonable limits. Situations and attitudes change over the course of a relationship, and you may find alternatives that work better for the two of you. There should be swift and certain consequences for violating the contract.

1. **Be fair, reasonable, and forgiving.** First, simply talk about the violation and determine if you can come to a reasonable agreement. The Mama's Boy wants your attention, so he may be willing to comply.

2. **There must be consequences for his behavior.** If that does not work, then you can decide how you will handle the infraction. It is okay to say calmly, "If you repeatedly refuse, ignore, or forget to cook on your night (manipulation), I will not cook for you. I will also have to reconsider cooking on my nights." A consequence must have teeth in it. As Mark Twain said, "The man that sets out to carry a cat by its tail learns something that will always be useful . . ."

   Simply saying, "You hurt my feelings" is unlikely to be particularly effective as a consequence. Never bluff. If you aren't certain you will follow through, don't threaten.

   Be prepared, he will have excuses. Remember, excuses have worked well for him in the past. It is your responsibility to be certain his excuses are no longer effective.

3. **Don't be swayed by excuses.** When you "see" positive change, then you can enthusiastically affirm his cooperative behavior. Affirmation at the appropriate time is an extremely powerful tool.

4. **Be consistent.** If you draw a line in the sand and then recapitulate, you will have accomplished nothing. If you say, "The next time you begin screaming, I will leave until we can speak calmly," do it. To be effective this must be your statement and your action every time he screams.

5. **Choose your battles carefully.** Decide what is most important to you and stand your ground around those issues. If you fight over every insignificant issue, you will turn your

relationship into a battleground. That strategy will eventually drive you crazy. Remember, you are still in control of your life when you choose not to do battle.

6. **Avoid the blame game.** He has been taught that nothing is his fault. Just because he says you are at fault (you obviously misunderstood what he said or are simply a nag) doesn't make it true. Don't respond to blaming. You cannot and do not cause him to do or feel anything. You have probably responded to blaming in the past. Did it help? I rest my case.

7. **There is strength in numbers.** Bounce your thoughts off friends and family without creating an "us against him" environment. You can become lost in his excuses, blaming, and attention-getting behaviors, or in the heat of battle. After a while, you may no longer be certain what is appropriate. Discuss your ideas and beliefs with friends who can be objective. Simply agreeing with you is not helpful.

A word of caution: You cannot take responsibility for changing his behavior. He must want to cooperate for the sake of the relationship. You have three choices in any relationship. (1) You can accept it as it is (I hope without upsetting yourself each time something happens). (2) You can change the relationship (you must have his cooperation for sweeping changes). (3) Or, you can leave the relationship. These comprise the limits of your power.

The Bottom Line

We have a choice: to plow new ground or let the weeds grow.
Jonathan Westover

If you have too many weeds in your garden, it may be time to reflect and reach for your hoe.

You have tried all of the strategies and he continues to choose his role as son over his role as husband, or to expect you to be his mother. He refuses to accept his share of the responsibility for your relationship and continues to deny, avoid, and excuse his manipulative behavior. It may be time to reconsider your commitment to him. Ask yourself if this relationship is working for you. Do you feel appreciated, respected, and loved? What percentage of the time are you happy you chose this man?

Keep a journal for at least one month. At the end of each day, rate your relationship enjoyment on a scale of one (miserable) to ten (exceedingly happy). If you have an average of five or less, you might want to decide if your relationship is healthy. In a healthy relationship, you receive enough support, affection, and nurturing to allow you to focus on growing as a human being. In an unhealthy relationship, you expend valuable time and energy attempting to pry your needs from your lover.

Making a life-altering decision is frightening. Take your time and talk about your concerns with a good friend. Also, a therapist could be very helpful while you explore your options.

The Mama's Boy Test

Do you have a Mama's Boy? Take the test.

1. Do you have to make most of the decisions?
    YES ◯   No ◯

2. Does he spend as much time with his mom as he does with you?
    YES ◯   No ◯

3. Is he afraid of being abandoned?
    YES ◯   No ◯

4. Does he believe that he is unique and deserves special treatment?
   Yes ○   No ○

5. Is he sensitive to criticism?
   Yes ○   No ○

6. Does he lack understanding and concern for others?
   Yes ○   No ○

7. Does he seem preoccupied with himself?
   Yes ○   No ○

8. Does he expect you to take more than your share of the responsibility for your relationship?
   Yes ○   No ○

9. Does he blame you or others for his mistakes?
   Yes ○   No ○

10. Does he have difficulty saying, "I am sorry"?
    Yes ○   No ○

11. Does he whine to get his way?
    Yes ○   No ○

12. Do they (your husband and his mother) gang up on you?
    Yes ○   No ○

13. Does his mother believe he is unusually special?
    Yes ○   No ○

14. Does he have a spotty employment record?
    Yes ○   No ○

15. Has he left jobs in a huff?
    Yes ○   No ○

16. Does he say he is not appreciated at work (on more than one job)?
    Yes ○   No ○

17. Is his mom his ideal of womanly behavior?
    Yes ○   No ○

18. Do you feel that you are competing with his mother?
    Yes ○   No ○

19. Does he manipulate the truth when it is serves his purpose?
    Yes ○   No ○

20. Has he been described as arrogant?
    Yes ○   No ○

21. Does he want you to mother him?
    Yes ○   No ○

22. Has that been a pattern in his life?
    Yes ○   No ○

Scoring the Test

Give one point for each yes answer.

Scores 1 to 7

He has some attributes that lean in the Mama's Boy direction. Happily for you, he is not yet at enough of an incline to be considered a Mama's Boy. I would suggest talking with him about your concerns. Choose a time when you will not be interrupted. Clearly state the behaviors you want from him. Be specific: "I want a kiss before you leave in the mornings" not "I want more affection." If you ask for the latter, he won't have a clue what to do differently.

Listen respectfully when he talks and indicate that you are listening by making encouraging sounds every once in a while (i.e., Yes, right, I see) and use good listening body language (i.e., lean forward, nod, smile encouragingly).

Good luck.

Scores 8 to 14

Your man is getting dangerously close to being a Mama's Boy. I am concerned; however, the score may be a misunderstanding. There is still hope for you. Try the advice I suggested for the former group. If that doesn't work, consult a couple's counselor. Therapy can be a very positive and empowering experience for you and your man.

A therapist is usually interested in the following information. However, her focus will depend on her theories on counseling.

- What works in your relationship? It would be a very unusual relationship if it had no positives. I believe in identifying the strengths in your relationship and building on them.
- Why did you choose this particular time to seek counseling? Why now?
- What are the top five issues that create distress?
- What attracted you to each other when you dated? Often the very traits that brought you together create problems later.
- What have you done to try to fix the problem? Frequently, current problems are merely former attempts to solve a problem.

Scores 15 to 22

I am afraid the news is not good. Either you seriously misgraded the test or your man is a Mama's Boy. Again, this is not the worst cluster of symptoms he could have. Reread the chapter and try the suggestions given to the former groups. The words you say and the tone in which you say them can make a beautiful difference in your life; stranger things have happened.

Here are three suggestions that have helped other couples and may be just what you need.

Tell your Mama's Boy that you have tried everything you know and you are at a dead end. Ask him what he would suggest to rejuvenate your marriage. Be very clear about what you will and will not do. This may be the wake-up call he has not heard from you in the past.

There are many fine retreats specializing in marriage (couple's) enhancement. Sign up for one in your area if he is willing to attend. Even if he is not enthusiastic about the idea, if he agrees to attend, he may start thinking differently about his responsibilities and how important your relationship is to him.

Begin to focus on yourself and your future without him. I have found that men often begin to pursue their lady when they realize that she is serious about leaving. Frequently, men simply do not believe you will carry through with your plans to leave. When they understand that the dissolution of your relationship is imminent, many decide to work with you toward a solution. This is not a ploy; you must be serious.

If, like a steadfast soldier, you try and your efforts succeed, you will gain much of great value. If not, you will be pleased that you gave it your best effort.

It is the time to contemplate your options. Again, your choices are as follows:

- Change the relationship (you need his cooperation)
- Accept the relationship
- Leave the relationship

You will decide which choice is appropriate for you and your circumstances. You have the right to be treated with love, respect, and kindness. They are not negotiable; they are a given. You deserve them—period. End of discussion.

I wish you success, together, in altering the patterns that have become the life you share with your partner.

Conclusion

Depending on his degree and number of symptoms, your Mama's Boy may be a workable choice. If you are a nurturing woman and are willing to share him with his mother, the relationship may be appropriate for you. We understand that perfect relationships are not an option. Don't we?

If you focus on your mate's positive characteristics and behaviors, you will experience more gratification in the relationship. Be sure to praise the behaviors you have requested; in fact, praise his attempts. He will enjoy the attention and will very likely repeat those behaviors. If you hope to ignore his mother, you will need iron determination reminiscent of Churchill's unwavering resolve as bombs detonated around him. You may want to ponder your resources for a while.

In this fast-paced, work all day world, you are bound to run into more than one of the next type of man . . . The Workaholic.

CHAPTER 3

The
Workaholic

People throw away what they could have by insisting on perfection, which they cannot have, and looking for it where they will never find it.
⌐ *Edith Schaeffer*

THE WORKAHOLIC'S IN A committed relationship with his Day Timer, laptop, and cell phone. You see him sitting in airports, impeccably dressed and keyboarding or animatedly arguing with his cell phone. He appears frazzled, as if someone has just trampled all over his shiny Gucci loafers. A Workaholic's career is "who he is" not "what he does." He may also perceive "what he has" as a defining element of "self." Needless to say, he takes his work very seriously.

I have seen this "work is God" mindset in police officers, especially if they are recent academy graduates. Their all-consuming zeal for law enforcement usually declines though the years and they become more mainstream. This is not the prognosis for most overachievers. Workaholics share much with individuals who meet the criteria for Obsessive-Compulsive Personality

Disorder (OCPD). This is not the same diagnosis as Obsessive-Compulsive Disorder (OCD), the life-limiting condition made famous in James Brooks' *As Good As It Gets* starring Jack Nicholson. OCD individuals may have compulsive behaviors such as checking fifty times to be certain the front door is locked before leaving for work. As you can readily understand, these behaviors interfere with the OCD sufferer's relationships and career. Whereas, the defining features of OCPD is a tendency to be perfectionist, inflexible, and preoccupied with orderliness.

Workaholics miss much of the fun in life. They simply don't have the time for their families and friends, hobbies, physical activity and restorative relaxation, or so they will swear to you. Actually, they have the same twenty-four hours as you and I. Work, which is not only laudable, but decidedly necessary for most of us, becomes the driving force in their lives. A career can be a voraciously demanding lover and taskmaster.

Some experts will insist that this commitment to a career is pathological. These experts may say Workaholics are insecure and unable to face life; consequently they hide behind their work. This may be quite true of some workaholics, but human beings are exceptionally complex creatures. There are no uncomplicated answers that will always apply. Enthusiastic workers may gain a great deal of satisfaction from their art or the services they perform. Counselors, clergy, physicians, and artists might fall into this category. Many of the manipulative types crave attention. They might become actors, attorneys, clergy, musicians, politicians and/or "the expert" in any field. Naturally, not all or even most of these illustrious professionals are manipulators or consummate attention junkies. Also, a profession may fit into more than one category (i.e., clergy). Human beings will invest their time and effort wherever we receive the biggest payoff. The payoff may be anything we value, such as increased self-esteem, power, money, attention, fame, altruism (. . . does it then qualify as altruism?) or simple enjoyment.

Workaholics cross the line and the venerable work ethic becomes a destructive obsession or addiction. Do you know a Workaholic? Is your man married to his Palm Pilot? Perhaps, you find yourself sitting, tapping your foot and looking at your watch wondering where he is on too many long forlorn nights. Do you worry that he won't show for family functions? Does dinner get cold and dry because he comes home much later than promised? Do you have to drug him and tie him to the bumper of the car before he will go on a long weekend or vacation?

You may have a Workaholic. Let's find out.

Criteria for the Workaholic

The Workaholic is easy to identify. You will know by the time you finish reading the criteria if your man has gone beyond enthusiastic worker into driven Workaholic.

- He is the first one at work
- He is the last to leave
- He regularly brings work home
- Most social occasions involve work
- Most of his "friends" are coworkers
- He promises to be home in time for dinner for two, but seldom follows through
- If he takes a vacation he frequently checks in with his coworkers or employer
- His conversations usually revolve around his work
- He frequently eats meals at his desk
- He takes business calls after hours

- He says he will cut back on his hours, but it never happens
- He wants his performance to be "perfect"
- The only "right way" is his way
- He is inflexible
- He won't delegate work unless it will be done his way
- He is overly concerned about rules, schedules, lists, and organization

If your mate has five or more of these traits he is probably overcommitted to work. His commitment is likely causing problems in his personal relationships. His health may be suffering because of a poor diet, lack of exercise, alcohol consumption to reduce stress and/or insufficient time to relax.

Two of the most common types of workaholics are the Holy Grail Seeker (HGS) and the Overburdened Procrastinator (OP). The HGS believes that perfection exists "out there" and he must find it. He looks for it in every assignment, every project and every mission. It doesn't matter to the HGS that perfection takes a great deal of time (infinity) and the Holy Grail is unattainable. The dedicated HGS continues to seek in vain. He spends numerous long hours refining and improving. He needs the advice I was given when I was wading through the dissertation process. A professor at Emory University whispered the secret to graduating in my ear, "There are two types of dissertations. One is perfect, the other is finished."

The Overburdened Procrastinator takes on too many projects because he cannot say no, or he thinks he is the only one who can complete the job correctly. He can't designate, because coworkers are unable to meet his lofty standards. He is like the frazzled mother who won't allow her young child to stir the cake batter, because he might make a mess. For the OP there is only one right way—and it is his way. Therefore, he accepts projects before he has finished current assignments. His desk "floweth" over.

He may relish a challenge and the adrenaline flow that follows. Some men are trapped in jobs that require a great investment of time and they cannot see satisfactory options.

Again, human beings refuse to fit nicely into little labeled cubby holes. Each workaholic burns the midnight oil for reasons that are uniquely his. Generalizations help us to better understand certain behaviors, but they do not give us a map with a giant "X" on it.

The Workaholic and the American Work Ethic

Americans are a hardworking, ambitious people. We work longer hours than most Europeans and we take off fewer days. Research studies indicate that many of us never take vacations.

Companies explored the ideal balance of work and life responsibilities as early as the 1930s. The "W.K. Kellogg Company created four six-hour shifts to replace the traditional three daily eight-hour shifts" (Lockwood, 2003, p. 2). The Kellogg Company reported an increase in employee spirits and competence, possibly because employees were less fatigued or enjoyed more leisure time. However, eighty years later the work ethic is still very much alive in the hearts of many Americas. We admire and respect individuals who are productive and hard working. However, this may be somewhat gender specific. Men are admired for providing well for their families. Women who are ambitious and work oriented may be criticized for neglecting their husbands and children.

However, it appears that both genders may feel guilty when their work life steals time from family obligations. In a study by Rutgers University (2001), most working adults were concerned

> **Did you know** there is a dating service for busy executives (workaholics)? Yes, there is, it is called It's Just Lunch. After paying a rather hefty fee ($1000 to $1500), staff do all of the footwork, arrange the "lunch" and coordinate busy schedules. Members can remain firmly affixed to their keyboards or telephones until the entire meeting has been orchestrated. I wonder how many of the members actually attend the first meeting. This illustrates the theory that our culture supports the workaholic ethic. There are many such successful services just waiting for the overachiever (or his/her secretary) to pick up the phone. ☞

that they were not spending enough time with their families. This is encouraging news for the partner of an overachiever.

Case Study #1: Bobby and Denise

Bobby and Denise have been married for four years. They have a one-year-old daughter, Lauren. They are twenty-eight and this is the first marriage for both. Bobby is a slightly overweight attorney with a large firm. His firm specializes in worker injuries. He has worked there since he graduated from law school. Denise works at a private school for gifted children, tutoring in conversational Russian. She chose to work part-time after Lauren was born. Denise had hoped that she and Bobby would be the Waltons. However, Denise has been disappointed by Bobby's zealous devotion to the American work ethic. She had envisioned him spending long romantic hours in front of the fireplace with her, and playing and reading bedtime stories to little Lauren.

She asked Bobby to come home for dinner as often as possible. Denise believes families should share their day with each other at the dinner table. Her mother and father were emphatic about gathering for dinner; no excuses were allowed. Bobby usually arrives home in time for dinner every couple of weeks. She and Lauren eat alone or go to her parent's home. He normally eats at work with other ambitious young attorneys in his firm. He is terrified that the senior partners might notice an empty chair at his desk.

Bobby and Denise have not taken a vacation together since their honeymoon. Denise has been beseeching Bobby to take a long weekend to go to Disney World. He keeps putting her off saying he has too much work to do. He insists, "You don't make partner by going to Disney World." He complains that she doesn't take his work seriously enough and she is trying to hold him back. Their love life has gone into a downward spiral. He is too tired for lovemaking and she is too despondent.

Denise has asked him to go to couple's counseling with her. He refused saying, "There is nothing wrong with me. I am trying to get ahead so I can give you and Lauren the good things in life. I am the one paying all the bills. Grow up for god's sake!" Denise feels unheard and unappreciated. She is seriously considering filing for a separation. Interestingly, Bobby also feels unheard and unappreciated.

Bobby's Manipulative Techniques

Blaming: "There is nothing wrong with me." If there is nothing wrong with Bobby, then their arguments must be Denise's fault. He also attempts to avoid blame by turning around and blaming Denise.

You are unreasonable: "Grow up for god's sake!" Bobby implies, rather strongly, that Denise is immature, and if she would only think like an adult she would understand.

Empty promises: He makes promises to change, but never follows through. He uses this popular manipulation rather than working with Denise to find solutions to their issues.

You are not important: "I am the one paying all the bills." In other words, why is she bothering him with details? He is the bread winner, brings home the bacon, and is important. Obviously, what she wants is not important.

Bobby and Denise are not without options. Generally, a Workaholic can be persuaded that change is necessary and part of that change will be his responsibility, especially if he fears losing his family. Since Bobby refuses to go to therapy, it would be a good idea for Denise to go alone. In this case, her goal would be to learn how to approach Bobby in ways that are effective and do not further harm an already fragile relationship. A word of caution, if one seeks individual therapy and grows as a person and the spouse does not, the relationship may suffer. Denise should discuss this risk with the therapist during the first session.

Karen and Charles are also vigorously discussing work and relationship commitments. Let's listen in on their rather heated conversation.

Case Study #2: Charles and Karen

Karen and Charles have been living together for two years. They work at a large urban automobile dealership. They were classmates in college and started dating in their senior year. Karen is a tall, slim brunette and Charles is redheaded six-footer. She is a successful salesperson and he is the overcommitted finance officer. Karen has many interests. She works her forty hours and goes home to read, talk to friends, bake luscious desserts or run with her German Shepherd. When they were dating, Charles enjoyed doing these things with her. They also went to all the good movies and attended theater performances.

As is usual when beginning new careers, both Karen and Charles were enthusiastic employees. They arrived at work early, learned all they could and left reluctantly at the end of each day. After a few months, Karen began to settle into a routine and spent more time on her interests. Charles lurched the other direction and spent more and more time in his small, cramped office. Karen frequently called him to ask when he was coming home. He would say, "It will be just a few minutes, I am almost finished." It was never a few minutes and she would call back again.

She grew frustrated with trying to have a relationship with a ghost. Karen began to believe she was the only one interested in their relationship. Charles always had excuses. Excuses did

Couples Therapy at the Movies: When I saw her in counseling (to resolve lingering pain) her story reminded me of the Charles Dickens' Yuletide classic, *A Christmas Carol*. As you may remember, young Scrooge lost the woman he loved when he became immersed in accumulating wealth. Later, as he reflected on his past (at the behest of the Ghost of Christmas Past), losing "that gentle creature" was one of his most agonizing regrets. Karen decided to buy the film and watch it with Charles as her last desperate effort before walking away. Miracles happen, the timeless story worked its magic and Charles at last began to understand the price he was paying for the privilege of working himself to death. His transformation was not spectacular, but it was sincere and it was a beginning. ☢

not keep Karen warm at night. Her frustration grew into anger and Charles became resentful. He told her not to call him at work. He said, "I will be home when I get home . . . don't interrupt me." His share of the household chores was seldom, if ever, completed. Karen carried the entire responsibly for maintaining their apartment, cooking, and buying groceries. When she confronted Charles about the inequity in their relationship he accused her of nagging. He reminded her that his salary was stable; her salary depended on sales. This is a very popular ploy.

After months of Charles' denial, avoidance, and anger, Karen decided to look for another job and leave the relationship. She resolved to end the relationship now, rather than later after they were married and possibly had children. Though it was a very painful decision, Karen wanted children and she had no desire to be both mother and father.

CHARLES' MANIPULATIVE TECHNIQUES

Tantrum: "I will be home when I get home . . . don't interrupt me." An angry Charles' message to Karen was, if converted to a child's language, "Go away, I'm having fun. You always ruin my fun."

Avoidance: Charles chose to pretend they had no problems. If Karen wished to face reality, she would have to do it alone. This is also *blaming* . . . it means, if there is no problem, then you must have invented this issue just to be annoying.

Ignoring: When possible, Charles pretended she wasn't there.

Shirking responsibility: Working long hours does not mean that Charles is absolved of his responsibility for household chores. He chooses to work long hours. "I am busy" or

"I make more money than you" are bold attempts to convince Karen that she should take sole responsibility for cleaning and other chores. This is also a form of arrogance.

Starring the Workaholic

We have an "embarrassment of riches" when searching for famous Workaholics. Let's begin with the overachieving funny man and fledgling writer, Peter Sellers. He was so busy that he slept only four hours a night. Sellers starred in numerous movies, including the highly successful and hilarious Pink Panther series. He worked ten years to bring his last movie, *Being There . . .* to the big screen. For his efforts, he won a Golden Globe award and an American Academy Award nomination. Unfortunately, he died the following year of a heart attack. He was married four times.

Let's take a trip back into time to the French Golden Era, when Frenchmen glowed with pride in their leader, Napoleon Bonaparte, Emperor of the Empire. Incredibly, he created an Empire that heavily influenced Europe for more than 100 years, on four hours of sleep each night. Napoleon was much too busy conquering nations to waste precious time dozing. In spite of his military brilliance, political savvy, strategic genius, demanding schedule, and scant sleep, he toppled from power in 1815. According to historian, Robert Wilde (2003), "He couldn't be everywhere within his empire at once, and the forces he sent to pacify Spain failed, as they often did elsewhere." Perhaps he was not good at delegating, a problem for many workaholics. The last straw floated down when his army was decimated in a horrific Russian winter struggle. In all fairness to his enemies, he left with 400,000 troops (a number unheard of in his era) and returned with 10,000. He had the workaholic's drive and limited long-term planning. Napoleon was banished to St. Helena Island where he died at 1821. He was married twice and home very little.

Famous inventor Thomas Edison was, by all accounts, an enthusiastic workaholic, in fact, his entire team was known for keeping an exhausting schedule. However, after his first wife died he became smitten with a lovely eighteen-year-old. So much so that he could not even navigate the streets safely. According to his diary, "Saw a lady who looked like Mina. Got thinking about Mina and came near being run over by a streetcar. If Mina interferes much more will have to take out an accident policy" (Beal, 1999). Later in his life, after the glow wore off, "he spent a shockingly small amount of time with his family." From this we learn that a smitten lover is not necessarily a devoted husband.

Dealing with the Workaholic

Individuals with OCPD and workaholics are not unlikable or deceptive by nature. Generally, they won't steal your jewelry, fabricate a "façade" personality, profess undying love that also does not exist or get busted on drug charges on your first date. They have issues with perfectionism and moderate (sometimes severe) inflexibility, but they are not cast in iron . . . they will often yield somewhat if they see a reasonable necessity. We need to understand what the Workaholic admires and respects. Workaholics admire conscientiousness, tenaciousness, precision, achievement, independence and, perhaps, appreciation. They are list makers extraordinaire, rational and logical in their thinking processes . . . most of the time. Of course, it is their special interpretation of rational and logical thinking. Therefore, let's give them some lists and rational guidelines.

The following conflict resolution technique is very effective in creating a satisfactory compromise. However, it is complicated and rather daunting to feelers . . . thinkers love it. Your workaholic will see that you have done your homework and may decide to participate in resolving some relationship issues.

Bobby and Denise have been arguing about taking a three-day trip to Disney World. As you may remember, they have not taken a trip since their honeymoon, four years ago. They are using our conflict resolution technique to reach a compromise that will work for both of them. That means each will walk away from their compromise efforts feeling heard and appreciated. It does not mean each will get what he or she wants.

Dr. McCoy's Conflict Resolution Technique

Denise's Position	Bobby's Position	Options
Take off three days and go to Disney World next weekend	Go next year (12 months from now)	1) Take an overnight trip to Sea World this weekend. 2) Go to Sea World this weekend; go to Disney World in 6 months. 3) Go to Disney World next month; don't discuss trips again for 6 months

They began by clearly stating what they want. The statements should be as detailed as necessary to help the other person understand what is wanted. After they discussed their current positions on the issue they sought options that would include some part of what each of them wanted. The more options you generate the better. Then apply the criteria for a "good" compromise to each option.

Good Option Criteria

Acceptability—Do both parties feel good about the solution? If Denise or Bobby has to be bullied into a solution kicking and screaming, it is not an acceptable solution.

Practicality—Denise and Bobby might agree that taking a world cruise would provide good, quality family time together. However, if the cruise takes a month and costs 50 percent of their annual budget, it may be better to continue looking for that elusive "perfect" solution. Besides, if Bobby agrees to this he is probably feverish.

Equitability—How fair is the solution? One of the partners may be very accommodating at that moment for various reasons. Nonetheless, one-sided solutions lead to resentment.

Mutual involvement—Have both partners enthusiastically contributed to creating options? Each partner should contribute approximately 50 percent of the suggestions. Otherwise he or she may not feel invested in the process and will be less likely to follow through.

RANKING

Each partner can rank each solution on a scale of one to four. This will add more precision to the process. Perfectionists are exceedingly fond of precision.

4—*strongly support this option*
3—*support this option*
2—*do not support this option*
1—*hate this option*

For example, Denise and Bobby have created three options (more is better).

	Option 1	Option 2	Option 3
Denise	4	2	1
Bobby	4	1	3

In this case, both Bobby and Denise have given their highest mark to the first option. If this were not the case, then they would need to discuss the options again. At this point it is important to understand why they liked or disliked an option. Further compromise might be necessary. Again, the most important aspect of this or any conflict resolution technique is feeling good about the process. Each partner should feel heard and appreciated. If this technique is to work it is essential to follow the ground rules.

CONFLICT RESOLUTION GROUND RULES

Give each partner equal time to state his or her position
Do not argue with partner's statement
Do not raise your voice
Do not assign blame
Do not defend yourself
Avoid sarcasm, impatience, and taunting
Listen with a loving ear
Support some part of your partner's statement (even if it is just,
    "I can see this is important to you")
Do not drag the hurtful past into the process

Let's look at the characteristics the Workaholic admires and respects again. Sometimes we must enter a mate's reality in order to communicate with him. In his world tenacity, precision, perfection, conscientiousness, achievement, and appreciation are words to live by. We can use these traits to "reach" the overachiever.

Precision, Perfection. If you want to make a point with your mate, you had better have your ducks in a row. Think about what you want from him and express it in very concise language. In fact, writing it down is a good idea. Presentation is essential in the business world ... make it look neat, organized and easy to read and understand. He may give you a grade on it.

Tenacity. He doesn't give up easily (if ever), why should you? Show appreciation for his "can do" spirit at work and tell him you feel the same way about your relationship. He will respect a controlled, consistent approach. He may not agree to anything you ask, but he will respect you.

Achievement. You are achieving goals in your life, tell him about them. You may not have thought of your experiences as "achievement" but after giving it some thought, you will find areas in which you have excelled. If you have always wanted to take a class, volunteer or learn a new skill, this might be a good time to follow through. Achievement will make your life more satisfying and bolster your self-esteem.

Appreciation. He may overwork to gain approval and feel worthy. You might point out his worthy characteristics, especially if they are not related to work. We are drawn to people who make us feel good about ourselves. Sincere approval for the person he is and the family-related tasks he performs will draw him toward you, the source of unconditional approval.

Also, working together to tune-up your marriage or relationship is an achievement for both of you.

1. **Be fair, reasonable, and forgiving.** Only ask for the achievable, he will probably never be Brad Pitt no matter how much you may deserve Brad. Changing a relationship is a two-way street. There will be little annoyances he wants eliminated

or contained. Acknowledge your absence of sainthood and willingly agree to consider alternative behaviors. The most flexible, committed person goes first . . . if you are that person; just don't call this detail to his attention. He will fail in some attempts to master new relationship skills and behaviors. Applaud the attempts. Forgive the occasional lapse.

2. **There must be consequences for his behavior.** Our learning is based on natural and logical consequences. If consequences are negative we are less likely to repeat a behavior. If consequences are positive we are more likely to repeat the behavior. This is a Behavioral Principle, taken from Behavior Theory. You might be surprised at how powerful this simple technique is. If consequences are natural, they follow one's behavior, as night follows day, without any assistance from one's mate. If I should decide to disengage reason and go outside without a coat in my beautiful North Carolina mountains in January, I am going to freeze. That is a natural consequence. Women often remove the consequences of a behavior they would like to extinguish. For example, if my husband worked late (frequently) and I faithfully postponed dinner so his food would still be palatable, I remove a negative consequence. Naturally, if the late night sessions are infrequent, it is reasonable and caring to delay dinner and eat with him.

3. **Don't be swayed by excuses.** There are literally hundreds of excuses for working late; he will probably know all of them. "Sorry, Hon, I will be working late because my desk was swept away by a tornado" says only one thing, "I will be working late." Be fair; check the Weather Channel just to be certain a tornado didn't pass through your area.

4. **Be consistent.** If you say you will or will not do something, follow through every time. He is probably well aware of the principles of negotiation. The first principle of negotiation is

. . . don't negotiate with someone you can't trust to keep his or her word. Rash threats fall on deaf ears. You know what the Texas Rangers say, "You can't beat a fellow who is in the right and keeps coming."

5. **Choose your battles carefully.** You don't want to live in a foxhole and neither does he. Start with something small and amendable to change and begin the negotiation process. Look into his eyes, smile, hold your head high, speak calmly, listen carefully, be patient, and think before you speak. You will feel and appear confident. Confidence wins battles.

6. **There is strength in numbers.** Keep the troops handy. Support from your friends will help you to feel strong and sustain your confidence. Your support system will also help you to maintain your sanity.

There is one important truism to remember, in a love relationship there will be two winners or two losers.

The Bottom Line

As with some of our other types, the Workaholic is trainable. He is accustomed to doing what needs to be done. If you decide to go to therapy he will probably work hard in sessions. Be consistent and gracious; thank him for attempts to move in the direction of his family. Even failed attempts should be praised. You will begin to see meaningful changes, unless he is a narcissist. In that case, read the chapter on narcissists. They are in an entirely different ballgame from the average Workaholic and a narcissist-specific approach is advisable. If you aren't sure, use the advice in this chapter first.

The Workaholic Test

Do you have a Workaholic? Take the test.

1. Is his reading material usually job related?
   Yes ◯   No ◯

2. How long is his workweek?
   a. approximately 40 hours ◯
   b. 50 –59 hours ◯
   c. 60 hours our more ◯

3. Does he frequently eat lunch at his desk?
   Yes ◯   No ◯

4. Does he frequently eat breakfast at his desk or grab a bis-cuit at McDonalds on the way to work?
   Yes ◯   No ◯

5. Is he normally the last person to leave work (right after the clean up crew)?
   Yes ◯   No ◯

6. Would he rather get a promotion than improve your sex life?
   Yes ◯   No ◯

7. Is he so connected to his work that they are joined at the hip?
   Yes ◯   No ◯

8. Does he frequently rearrange your home life to accommo-date his job?
   Yes ◯   No ◯

9. When you are enjoying family and friends, is he focused on work?
   Yes ◯   No ◯

10. Is he bringing more work home now than a year ago?
    Yes ○   No ○

11. In his heart of hearts does he believe, "I must succeed."
    Yes ○   No ○

12. Would he agree with this statement: "I have more work than I can possibly complete. I need more hours in the day.
    Yes ○   No ○

13. Would he agree with the statement, "If I worked fewer hours, I don't know what I would do with my spare time."
    Yes ○   No ○

14. Have you complained about his long hours?
    Yes ○   No ○

15. Does he believe, "If I don't do it, it will be done wrong?"
    Yes ○   No ○

16. Does he frequently break promises to accommodate his work schedule?
    Yes ○   No ○

17. Is he a perfectionist?
    Yes ○   No ○

18. Does he procrastinate in an attempt to perform tasks perfectly?
    Yes ○   No ○

19. Does he go to extremes to be organized?
    Yes ○   No ○

20. Could he be described as inflexible and rule oriented?
    Yes ○   No ○

(Adapted from *The Ultimate Book of Personality Tests*, McCoy, 2005)

Scoring the Test

Give one point for each appropriate, indicative answer. I determine which answers are indicative. It gives me a sense of power.

Answers

1) y, 2) c, 3) y, 4) y, 5) y, 6) y, 7) y, 8) y, 9) y, 10) y, 11) y, 12) y, 13) y, 14) y, 15) y, 16) y, 17) y, 18) y, 19) y, 20) y

Score 0

Your mate is independently wealthy or looking for a job. Or, if he is employed, he is very laid back and knows how to enjoy his time away from work. He doesn't allow work to blend into your family time. His boundaries are very obvious and he is highly unlikely to drift into workaholism.

Scores 1 to 7

He is hard working. Though, if he is not careful he could gradually slide into workaholism. Why not nip this in the bud? Suggest meeting for lunch and take a little walk? Eat your food on a park bench, near a fountain or wherever the atmosphere is inviting. Suggest leaving his work at the office, perhaps he will take the pledge and start leaving work were it belongs—at work. Talk with him (gently) about learning to be more laid back and relaxed. It is simple. The next time he wants to work overtime, ask him to ponder this thought, "When Gabriel blows the horn for me, will I feel at peace, assured that I had been there for the people I loved? Or, will I remember many long nights sitting alone at my desk." These suggestions are normally well received if you show genuine concern for him *and* appreciation for the things he does that are family oriented.

Scores 7 to 14

It appears that he may be in an advanced stage of overworking and underplaying. He might want to ask himself what price he is paying and is he willing to pay to feed addiction. What would it take to get unstuck? What are the obstacles to a little freedom and fun, not to mention, rewarding relationships? As Dr. Donald Wetmore says, "If it frustrates you that they don't allow laptops on a Ferris wheel, you may be a workaholic." Does that sound like him? If it does, learn to say "no." It is an easy word to remember and difficult to misunderstand. Make a list of the things that can bring pleasure to your relationship. Talk with him about your needs as his partner. Ask him to start incorporating them (at least two or three) into your couple's schedule each week. It could become a healthy habit.

Scores 15 to 20

He is just inches away from spontaneous combustion. Stand back, please. However, if he will discuss the test and his score with you, he has begun to explore life after work. This is a very good start. He should be commended.

He can learn about the different types of workaholism and how to overcome his tendency to deprive himself of relaxation and rejuvenation. Author Dr. David Posen suggests asking one's self, "Why am I doing this." He may be surprised at his answers. Does he know that he could actually be more productive if he took breaks to refresh and refuel? Now, he can repeat after me, "My name is _____and I am a Workaholic." There, that's the first step toward a healthful solution.

Conclusion

Men overachieve and risk their health, families, and friends for various reasons. Your mate may seek attention, an adrenaline surge, to feel worthy or he may simply love his work. He is probably amendable to change, if approached in a sensitive, caring way. There are advantages and disadvantages to loving a Workaholic. He will provide well, he has many valuable characteristics (i.e., tenacious, conscientiousness, firm) or he would not be successful. The disadvantages are also numerous (i.e., late nights, inflexible, stubborn, perfectionist). You may have noticed that the "good" and the "bad" traits are simply a matter of degree. A perfectionist can also be called conscientious. Perseverance, taken to an extreme becomes stubborn. Firm can cross the line into inflexible. You will have to decide where the dividing line lies.

Next, we will meet the Eternal Jocks. They are stuck in time, at the moment of their glory as high school or college athletes. They bloomed early and decided they were smitten by the glow of constant admiration. Now, they refuse to step one foot outside their field of dreams. If you are an avid sports fan, a relationship with an Eternal Jock might fit comfortably. You can learn how to motivate your Jock by using the same principles a coach uses on the field. This type of manipulator has one significant advantage; his team played an essential part in his life. Team spirit means he plays well with others; this is something that cannot be said about most of the other types. He values team loyalty.

You are part of his team. Rah, rah.

CHAPTER 4

The
Eternal Jock

Half the lies they tell about me aren't true.
ᴖ *Yogi Berra*

Eᴛᴇʀɴᴀʟ Jᴏᴄᴋs ᴄᴀɴ ʙᴇ very attractive to women. They are self-confident, accomplished storytellers, and probably in good physical condition. They normally have many friends and an active social life. What woman would not enjoy a buff, popular person? Is your partner an Eternal Jock? Let's learn more and then decide. What do we know about the Jocks? According to the popular media, Jocks are spoiled, loud, vulgar, aggressive womanizers. Jocks are believed to blossom early and then coast through life reliving their early glory. They are said to have a sense of entitlement and, in their slightly slanted perspective, still view themselves as the macho, privileged males they were in their brief early stardom.

The other perception of athletics, especially in junior high school, is conversely very positive. One reads that team sports teach self-sacrifice, discipline, and fair play, and that they discourage delinquency and keep adolescents off drugs. Therefore, it appears that participation in team sports works miracles for younger children. However, once they enter high school or college, there may be a spontaneous metamorphosis into arrogant, boisterous jerks.

An Eternal Jock will be easy to recognize. On your first date, he will amuse you with a blow-by-blow recreation of his astounding winning touchdown in the last two seconds of the most critical football game in history. From that point, you must decide if you wish to pursue this relationship. If you do, you might expect him to be self-involved, attention seeking, and a virtual football trivia database of knowledge. Now, you must understand that he will plan his social commitments according to the games scheduled for any particular sports season. If you also live for the excitement of the gridiron, you will enjoy his enthusiasm and match it with your own. Perhaps, if you were an athlete or cheerleader, you would be a complementary team player for our sports enthusiast.

An Eternal Jock may be a good choice if you wish to spend your remaining years listening to stories of his early glory. He will also regale you with the latest statistics for his special team and any others that may interest him. He will spend spellbinding hours telling you why the current team is only a pale shadow of "his" team. Those wimps don't know how to play! He will want to hang out on weekends with "the boys," who are also firmly stuck in 1985, 1989, or whenever. Eternal Jocks have a cognitive time machine, and the date never changes. If none of this frightens you and you are willing to be in an ongoing competition with televised sports, a Jock is the guy for you.

As a consequence of their effort to explore the theory that "sports build character," Drs. Andrew Miracle and Roger Rees wrote *Lessons of the Locker Room*. In it they say, "Generally, involvement in any extracurricular activity is a good thing. But Sports are not better than band or chorus. The danger is that the 'win at any cost' attitude becomes so significant that the potential positive benefits are overwhelmed" (*Psychology Today*, 1994). Research indicates that kicking goals, evading tackles, and hitting balls has little character-building potential. For athletes, there seems to be a mixture of positive and negative outcomes. In one of their own studies, Miracle and Rees tracked 1,600 high school boys, the results indicate that the Jocks had greater self-esteem and attached "greater value to academic achievement" than boys who were not involved in sports. However, the athletes' aggression and irritability levels were higher. Further, the Jocks scored lower in self-control and in "belief in the importance of being honest than nonjocks" (*Psychology Today*, 1994).

Criteria for the Jock

Jocks vary in much the same ways as everyone else, and their characteristics also differ from individual to individual. However, these are the most common characteristics of the Jock's personality:

- Successful athlete (or believes he was)
- Preoccupied with himself
- Need for admiration
- Sense of entitlement
- Lack of understanding or concern for others
- More aggressive than non-Jocks
- More irritable than non-Jocks
- Excessively involved in sports (watching, playing, retaining sports trivia; in fact, his leisure time is consumed by sport-related activities)
- Often relives his athletic glory days

- Insensitive
- Spends a lot of time with other Jocks
- Enjoys being the center of attention
- High self-esteem
- Womanizer (remember, Jocks like attention)

Five or more predictors—especially believing he was a successful athlete, often reliving his past glory, and displaying insensitivity—indicate a high likelihood that your mate is an Eternal Jock. If he has most of the traits listed, he is a Super Jock.

Let's look in on Jock Rocky and his girlfriend, Kelly.

Case Study #1: Rocky and Kelly

Kelly and Rocky met in college and have been together for ten years. Rocky is a car salesperson; he sells Hummers. His employer was an enthusiastic team supporter when Rocky played football for the State University. Although selling is not Rocky's strength (he is still looking for that), he stays at the dealership and basks in the fading admiration from his college days. Kelly is a landscaper with her own company. She is very proud of her company's achievements and credits the all-female crew for her success. She still sees the glow of accomplishment that Rocky enjoyed when they were classmates. Kelly was an adoring fan when they started dating. In the past few years, however, her adoration has begun to wear thin as she matured and Rocky remained essentially the same. He has become the Eternal Jock.

Kelly calls Rocky from work to confirm their plans for tonight (Friday).

KELLY: Hi, Sweetheart, what time would you like to meet tonight?

ROCKY: No can do, Babe. I just talked to Spike. You remember him; he was a teammate. Anyway, we decided to go to the old school's varsity game tonight. We should be back Saturday.

KELLY: Rocky, you must be kidding! We have had plans for weeks to attend the National Landscaping Awards banquet. My company's work has been entered for an award; I told you how important this ceremony is.

ROCKY: I didn't promise anything. Evidently, you were not listening. Just back off! You are always trying to push me into this girly, flower crap! Why don't you just stop! I will go where I want and do what I want.

KELLY: Rocky! Rocky! (But Rocky had already hung up.)

Rocky used the following manipulative techniques.

ROCKY'S MANIPULATIVE TECHNIQUES

Intimidation: He raised his voice and was verbally aggressive. Jocks are taught to intimidate.

Blaming: His message is that Kelly is a scheming, controlling female. "Evidently you were not listening!" He blames Kelly for not listening to him and for trying to control his behavior. He knows that the best defense is a good offense.

You are a shrew: "You are always trying to push me into this girly, flower crap!" His message is that no normal woman would be doing this to a man. Yeah, right, Rocky.

Threat of abandonment: He hangs up without saying goodbye or telling Kelly when he will be in touch. He sends a very clear message: "Push me and I will be gone."

Case Study #2: Kyle and Tammy

First, I noticed Kyle's size. Forty-five-year-old Kyle is enormous, with wide shoulders and bulky arms and legs. In contrast, he has started to go soft around the middle, as former athletes are prone to do. Thirty-eight-year-old Tammy is tall and slim with flaming red hair.

They have been married five years and have four children between them. Each spouse was married once before. Kyle is an insurance salesperson, and Tammy is an engineer with a telecommunications company. Kyle begins the session saying, "I don't know what she is so upset about. She is always harping about something. I spend some time with the guys, drinking a few brews and talking sports, or go with them to a game and I never hear the end of it. I have high blood pressure now, and I am certain it is due to her incessant nagging. Just tell her to stop."

Tammy counters, "He is always with the boys. I never see him unless he is glued to sports on TV. I could stand in front of the TV naked and he would not notice me. I feel abandoned and undesirable. Last month, he forgot all about my birthday and went to a bar with the guys. I am tired of being invisible."

"I wish I could be invisible," retorts Kyle. "Then maybe you would stop trying to control my life. The other guys don't have this problem with their wives."

"Yeah, right. I happen to know that most of them are divorced. They don't have wives!"

Sports widowhood was the primary reason that Tammy and Kyle argued and decided to try therapy. They concurred, if they could conquer this issue in their marriage it would improve dramatically.

Each of them was harboring an illogical belief. Kyle thought he could live the same lifestyle he'd lived as a twenty-year-old college football player and bachelor. Tammy believed she could change Kyle if she put enough effort into it. After a couple of sessions, Tammy agreed to live her life to the fullest and let Kyle work on becoming a husband and father. Kyle reluctantly admitted that he loved his wife and agreed to begin the transition. Within four months, Kyle bid the guys adieu and came home after work to spend time with his family. On weekends, the happy couple planned enjoyable activities for the entire family. I was pleased to discover that Tammy and Kyle also found time to turn up the flame on their sexual relationship.

Kyle was stuck in his glory days and did not want to disturb his illusion. The days of ballgames and cheerleaders were gone; he is a middle-aged man with a family. He discovered that being a parent and spouse could also be exciting and rewarding. The thrill of scoring the winning touchdown now is simply a memory, no matter how real it may have seemed to Kyle.

Kyle and Tammy's story had a happy ending because they were committed to their relationship, even with its scars. When they began counseling, they were living in alien, incompatible worlds. Tammy could not enter Kyle's illusion, and Kyle didn't want to become a part of Tammy's reality. But Kyle had to shatter his past illusions of eternal youth and hero status in order to become a contributing dad and husband in the present.

KYLE'S MANIPULATIVE TECHNIQUES

You are a shrew: "The other guys don't have this problem with their wives." Kyle was giving Tammy the message that she was being unreasonable. His "one of the boys" behavior was perfectly acceptable, but her "shrewish" expectations were way out of bounds.

Whining: "I have high blood pressure now, and I am certain it is due to her incessant nagging." This Jock is beginning to sound like his Woe-Is-Me manipulative brothers. Of course, Kyle is saying, "Poor me, look what you have done to me."

Blaming: Kyle's first two techniques are also blaming. He is using the old manipulative gold standard: "I didn't do it. If I did do it, it was your fault."

As you have probably noticed, the manipulations are meant to distract you from the topic of the conversation. Attorneys will tell you that if you have a strong case, you plead your case; if not, you distract the opposition. When you stop to answer each of his accusations, you are playing the game. You are not required to defend yourself. You must simply turn the conversation back to the original topic.

Starring the Eternal Jock

University of Southern California coach John McKay said of his star player: "He was not only the greatest player I ever had—he was the greatest player anyone ever had. His NFL achievements included most rushing yards gained in one season, most rushing yards gained in a single game, and most touchdowns scored in a season." Who is this Super Jock? OJ Simpson is the most notorious example of a venerated athlete who chose not to accept the word *no.* According to surveys, most Americans believe Simpson and his Dream Team overpowered the opposition and dodged a double murder conviction. Fortunately, OJ Simpson is the exception. Eternal Jocks may be egocentric, but they are rarely cold-blooded killers.

According to former sportswriter Steve Dougan, Jocks have a "perception of invulnerability." They are accustomed to winning against all odds. Jocks may feel that they are entitled to the adoration of teachers, parents, coaches, and fans. Their perception of the real world is skewed and unrealistic. Perhaps society is to blame for eliminating consequences, and thus, their opportunities to learn from their mistakes. Jocks are pampered and cushioned from life's unpleasant realities as long as they consistently drop the ball in the little hoop or kick it between the goal posts.

The media has brought a lot of attention to athletes in every sport who have children out-of-wedlock and then disappear from their lives. Shawn Kemp was the poster boy, and he became a joke on the late-night show circuit because of it. While still in his twenties, he allegedly had ten children by eight women. He is not alone. In 1996, it was learned that "several Cowboys players had reportedly shared the expenses of a large rental house in suburban Dallas for weekly trysts with women and to do drugs" (Ball, ESPN, 2001).

Dealing with a Jock

Jocks are not lost causes. In most cases, they can make the changes necessary to maintain an intimate relationship. If your mate also has a personality disorder (i.e., psychopath, antisocial), then you are probably in for a prolonged, painful, and ultimately losing struggle. Jocks are amendable to the same rules as the other types in this book.

You have to know what you want changed and be able to describe it clearly in terms of the specific "behaviors" you are targeting. If you say, "Jock, you don't pay attention to me anymore and that makes me sad," there is a very good possibility that he will continue to pay scant attention. It is more effective if you follow the following formula.

1. Express your displeasure.
2. Specify his unwanted behavior and how you feel when he does "it."
3. Tell him what you would like instead.
4. Explain the consequences (perhaps the most important step).

Example

"Jock, you went out with the guys drinking four nights this week. I felt alone. I would appreciate it if you would spend at least six nights at home with me."

Important: Only add consequences if you have given him sufficient time to comply and he expresses no interest in cooperating.

Consequences: "I will plan my evenings with friends and family." If he is healthy enough (emotionally and psychologically) and cares about you, he will start to get the picture. Do not expect his behavior to change immediately. However, if he is making progress in the right direction, praise him. After all, Jocks crave attention. This is your opportunity to provide it.

Follow through with consequences: Always keep your promises. If he does not make any effort to meet your needs, then apply the consequences.

Relapse: If he makes progress and then returns to his good-old-boy lifestyle, begin making your evening plans without him again.

Write it down: Write down everything you have asked for, including all of the steps. Be very specific. Make sure to include everything he agrees to do. Both you and your mate should have a copy. Guard yours like the treasure it is.

Remember, he is accustomed to winning; your relationship should not become a tug of war. He can probably tug longer and harder than you. Be polite, be consistent, and do what you say you will do. Begin with the small, easy requests. When you resolve one issue, move on to the next one.

1. **Be fair, reasonable, and forgiving.** Do what his coach did: Tell him exactly what you want, and draw a diagram. Wait to see if he is interested in being a team player. Be sportsmanlike, fair, reasonable, and forgiving in the early stages of behavior change.

2. **There must be consequences for his behavior.** He learned in training camp to be a team player and to work for the good of the team. This learned behavior can be used in creating consequences; emphasize the benefit of the changes to your relationship team.

   Star basketball player Michael Jordan said, "I never looked at the consequences of missing a big shot . . . when you think about the consequences you always think of a negative result." We hope that your Jock will be willing to consider the consequences in your relationship.

3. **Don't be swayed by excuses.** Coaches hammered Jocks from an early age to produce results rather than give excuses. He has been prepared to give his best effort. Indeed, going the extra mile and "winning one for the Gipper" became a pattern, almost a religion, when he was playing his sport. Without this attitude, he would not have been a successful athlete. He will expect the same from you. Jocks can become team players at home if they understand the reasons for changing their behaviors rather than making excuses.

4. **Be consistent.** Athletes have been taught to be consistent in their performance. They fully appreciate the value of consistency. Your Jock will probably respect you more if you stick to your guns. He must understand that you are serious and that you will not simply give up if the going gets rough. If you say, "I will make plans to spend evenings with my family and friends," you must do it.

Consistency is important, but flexibility is also a tool in improving your relationship. Be prepared to change your plan when it is advantageous. Romantic relationships thrive in a compassionate, affectionate, generous, passionate, loving, and sympathetic environment. Therefore, your loving behaviors and emotions should be as consistent, if not more consistent, than undesirable consequences. When in doubt, say, "Don't make me come over there and love you."

5. **Choose your battles carefully.** Decide what is most important to you and stand your ground around those issues. If you fight over every little situation, you will turn your relationship into a battleground. That strategy will eventually drive you crazy. Remember, you are still in control of your life when you *choose* not to do battle.

Jocks were taught to fight all of the battles, not just the ones they believe they can win. You are not a Jock; so, it is okay to say to yourself, "No, I don't want to waste energy on this issue. I will wait for something more important to me."

If they are to endure, relationships must grow strong enough to weather an occasional hurricane. Human conflict is inevitable, and it is a fact of married life. You are not your partner; you are a unique human being with individual beliefs, behaviors, and goals. Conflict can be agonizing; accusations and hurtful words may be hurled in every direction. When we are hurt, angry, or frightened, running away may appear to be the most attractive choice. But stop for just a moment. What if you are meant for each other?

6. **Avoid the blame game.** Your Eternal Jock has been taught that nothing is his fault; he has a sense of entitlement. Jocks are accustomed to not being held to the same standards (except on the field) as mere mortals. Therefore, he may take the *offensive* and blame you. Before you accept blame, take the time to explore the situation and do a reality test with friends.

It is not helpful or particularly pleasant to defend yourself all the time. Try to resist playing that game; keep going back to your original point. You won't score any points if you are running all over the field (he knows that). Blaming one's partner rather than scrutinizing one's own behavior is counterproductive.

It is easy to become confused when the person we love blames us for his misfortune. Some of his arguments may even sound almost logical. Soon, we wonder why this is happening; we have never caused so much pandemonium in a person's life before. Then we say, "Hey, wait a moment. I can't be responsible for everything. I am not that powerful."

7. **There is strength in numbers.** Bounce your thoughts off friends and family without creating an "us against him" environment. You can become lost in his excuses, his blaming you, and his attention-getting behaviors, or you can lose your way in the heat of battle. After a while, you may no longer be certain what is appropriate. Discuss your ideas and beliefs with friends who can be objective; simply agreeing with you is not helpful.

Having good friends and family with whom to interact is more than just warm and fuzzy. It is healthy. A relationship that is experiencing upheaval is very stressful. In the Good

Health Practices Study of 6,000 individuals over six years, the results suggest that "those people who had poor social networks and support were two to three times more likely to die (2.3 times for men, 2.8 times for women) during the study than those persons with strong social support systems" (Vanderbilt Health Plus, revised September 30, 2005). If your support system is anemic, now is the time to give it a boost. Contact old friends, join a club, volunteer, attend religious services, or just stay in touch with friends and family.

The Bottom Line

If you have tried and nothing seems to make a difference, it may be time to explore your relationship and what it means to you. You can do this by making a list of the positives and negatives.

Relationship Positives	Relationship Negatives
He helps with the housework.	He won't spend cuddle time with me.
He is supportive when I am down.	He won't cut the grass.
He helps the kids with their homework.	He is gone most evenings.
He is successful professionally.	He never compliments me.
He loves my parents.	He hates my friends.
He is a good father.	He can't keep a job.
He is fun to be with.	He is always in a hurry.
He is a great lover.	He won't do anything nonsexual with me.
He has a good sense of humor.	In private, he loses his sense of humor.

If you would like to be more precise, when you finish your list give a value to each positive and negative item on the list. The values will be 1 to 5:

1—*Not very important*
2—*Slightly important*
3—*Important*
4—*Very important*
5—*Extremely important*

Choose a value for each item, and then add up the points on both sides (positive and negative). This scoring system should give you a relatively accurate picture of your relationship. If the weeds in your garden surpass the flowers, it is probably time to see a couple's counselor.

The Jock Test

Is your mate an Eternal Jock? Let's take the test.

1. Does he spend more time with his sports friends than with you?
   YES ○   No ○

2. Was he a successful athlete in school (college or high school)?
   YES ○   No ○

3. Does he still wear his varsity athlete sweater to ballgames?
   YES ○   No ○

4. Does he spend much of his leisure time either watching or playing sports?
   YES ○   No ○

5. Does he still tell his old touchdown stories?
    Yes ○   No ○

6. Does he enjoy being the center of attention?
    Yes ○   No ○

7. Does he work out or otherwise keep in shape?
    Yes ○   No ○

8. Is he especially competitive?
    Yes ○   No ○

9. Has he had many sexual relationships (before or after your relationship)?
    Yes ○   No ○

10. Does he have a philosophy of entitlement (he deserves special treatment, or the rules do not apply to him)?
    Yes ○   No ○

Scoring the Test

Give one point for each yes answer. Total the points.

Scores 0 to 3

It is unlikely that your mate is a dedicated Jock. He may enjoy the thrill of the gridiron or the sound of the ball hitting a hoop rim, but he is still relatively average. The three most indicative questions are numbers 2, 3, and 5. If you answered yes to all three, he may be a Jock in sheep's clothing. However, he might also be willing to hear your concerns and make positive changes.

Scores 4 to 7

Your mate has a number of characteristics indicative of Jocks. He may be a full-fledged Jock or simply an enthusiastic fan. However, there is room for movement. He may be willing to listen and work with you for the betterment of the relationship. Since he is a good team player, he may be willing to join your team. Think about what team players value: optimal performance, team spirit, winning one for the Gipper (a touch of sentimentality), worthy competition, and loyalty. These are valuable traits, and they can be used to enlist his cooperation.

Scores 8 to 10

You are probably in love with a Jock. Since he is self-confident, outgoing, and entertaining (the football stories), you probably enjoy being with him. You had good reasons for choosing him. As his other less desirable traits surfaced, you may have had second thoughts. Relax, though, he can be the man you fell in love with. Yes, it will take a little work. Perhaps he would like to coach a Little League team instead of drinking with the boys. There are ways he can pursue his interest in sports and still be a dedicated husband and father. You may want to take that cheerleader's uniform out of mothballs.

Once again, let's look at what he has been taught to value and how these values can be used to improve your relationship:

Optimal Performance

If you have children, does your spouse know an outstanding father? For example, is there someone your mate admires for his ability to connect with his children? If your Jock does, this would be a good man for him to emulate. What about your Jock's father? What did he learn from his father (or father figure) that is positive? What did he learn that he does not want to repeat with his children? You can't force him to learn from other fathers or husbands, but you can point him in that direction and allow him to carry the ball. This same technique can also be applied to his role as a spouse.

What is important to a Jock? You can use these convictions to create a winning team.

Team Spirit

Aren't the two of you a team? The two members of a committed relationship are a very special team with plans to play together for life, not for a single season. Discuss your roles as team players with him. What do you expect of him? What does he expect of you? Are either of you letting down the team? Be sure to write your roles in a contract and post it where you both can see it.

Sentimentality

His desire as an athlete to "win one for the Gipper" means that he probably has a touch of sentimentality. Using your power as part of the team, tell him how you feel when he lets you down. Ask him how he feels under those circumstances. Tell him what your team means to you. Ask him what it means to him. Jocks are more accustomed to emotions than you would think. Have you ever seen a player sitting on the bench and crying after a game when his performance did not meet his standards? Almost certainly, he is feeling despondent because he let down his teammates. Coaches employ sentimentality if they believe it will improve performance. You can do the same.

Worthy Competition

Does he see you as worthy to compete against? Jocks admire strength and determination. When you draw a line in the sand and "hang in there," he will respect your power. He may not change, but you certainly have nothing to lose.

Loyalty

Loyalty is much like team spirit. Since he first played T-ball at age five, your Jock has been taught to play his very best game every single time he came to bat. Right along with that, he was taught always to cheer for his team. If he hadn't understood loyalty, it is unlikely he would have ever been successful. Coaches are powerful motivators. Read about some of the greats, such as Bear Bryant and Knute Rockne. You will learn what makes him tick and possibly how to make your team a winner.

Conclusion

You have examined the advantages and disadvantages of the Eternal Jock. Yes, he is a bit self-absorbed. During his formative years, he was taught that he was special because he could throw a football (or whatever) better than anyone in his hometown. His "special" status brought good grades, popularity, a letter sweater that every girl wanted to wear, and maybe a small gratuity under the table. Privilege was expected and provided.

Let's review his advantages as a mate. He is a team player, gregarious, and often sentimental. Lucky for you, he is probably trainable. After all, his coach trained him. His disadvantages are his obsession with anything one can throw, kick, or slam-dunk, and his allergy to mate, home, and hearth. His committed relationship may be with "the guys." Also, his need for adoration could motivate him to wander. Did I mention that the Eternal Jock is trainable? His disadvantages can be overcome if he chooses to make changes for the Gipper and the home team. Rah, rah, rah.

Jocks are quite confident in certain areas, whereas our next manipulator is constantly fearful of looming defeat and abandonment. The Dependent Man sees catastrophe around every corner and under every rock. He believes someone should be there to assume responsibility, to guide him through decisions, to help him contain inevitable disasters. In his world, he is standing on a precipice and the ground is quaking beneath his feet. Are you willing to don your cape and rush in to save the day? Saving him may become a way of life. On a positive note, the Dependent Man and the Jock have something in common. They are capable of working toward more mutually satisfying relationships. The Dependent Man values your relationship. His most terrifying nightmare is abandonment. Let's nudge him away from the edge for a moment and meet the Dependent Man.

CHAPTER 5

The Dependent Man:
The Woe-Is-Me Complex

All charming people have something to conceal, usually their total dependence on the appreciation of others.
 Cyril Connolly

THE DEPENDENT MAN is a magnet drawing us closer. Caring, maternal women (most of us) want to save him, cheer him up, and help him discover his self-confidence. We are certain it is in there somewhere, and we can magically draw it forth. He looks so sad, and he certainly needs reassurance. He is a welcome safe harbor away from men who are aggressive, such as most of the other manipulative types. The Dependent Man, using the *DSM-IV-TR* criteria for Dependent Personality Disorder, is the epitome of congenial agreeableness. He respects our opinions, asks for our advice, and actually accepts our suggestions. You are wondering why is he a manipulator because he sounds great. Remember when we talked about taking neutral or positive traits to the extreme? Let's pull out our magnifying glass and take a closer look at the Dependent Man.

Positive or Neutral Trait	Extreme Trait
He asks for our opinion.	He has no opinions.
He asks for our advice.	He can't make independent decisions.
He is not aggressive.	He can be passive to a fault.
He needs us.	He can suck us dry.
He values us.	He won't let go.

Now, perhaps you see the disadvantages inherent in a man with Dependent Personality Disorder or with those tendencies. Your man will probably fall somewhere between positive and extreme. As with all of our manipulative types, approximately 90 percent of men will not meet the criteria for a personality disorder diagnosis. Your man may well have many of these traits; however, there are men who are dependent on their women who do not meet these criteria. We will discuss them briefly later.

Criteria for the Dependent Personality

The *DSM-IV-TR (2000)* defines Dependent Personality Disorder as a "pervasive and excessive need to be taken care of that leads to submissive and clinging behavior and fears of separation, beginning by early adulthood and present in a variety of contexts, as indicated by five (or more) of the following" criteria listed in the *DSM-IV-TR*:

- Has difficulty making everyday decisions without an excessive amount of advice and reassurance from others
- Needs others to assume responsibility for most major areas of his or her life
- Urgently seeks another relationship as a source of care and support when a close relationship ends

- Has difficulty expressing disagreement with others because of fear of loss of support or approval (this does not include realistic fears of retribution)
- Has difficulty initiating projects or doing things on his or her own (because of a lack of self-confidence in judgment or abilities rather than a lack of motivation or energy)
- Goes to excessive lengths to obtain nurturance and support from others, to the point of volunteering to do things that are unpleasant
- Feels uncomfortable or helpless when alone because of exaggerated fears of being unable to care for himself or herself
- Is unrealistically preoccupied with fears of being left to take care of himself or herself

The challenges are obvious. A Dependent Man "must" avoid being alone and making decisions; he abdicates responsibility for his life. Manipulation is simply a tool to secure the champion he covets. As with some other types, his crisis quickly becomes your crisis. The sky is perpetually falling in on him, and you have a sturdy umbrella. There are two warnings I should make: (1) Only a qualified professional can assess pathology, and (2) the vast majority of Dependent Men will not meet the full criteria for this disorder. That said, symptom severity is also important in determining how much the man's life (especially relationships) is impacted. It is possible to have fewer than five symptoms and have greater challenges than a man diagnosed with the disorder—if the symptoms are severe.

As we look at personality traits, such as dependency, we would do well to understand that the traits that enable us to fit successfully into our career "niche" might contribute to discontent in personal relationships. A Dependent Man might thrive in a job that valued direct supervision of employees. He would be very comfortable with micromanagement. Understanding this concept helps us to perceive individual characteristics in a less judgmental manner.

For example, if you meet a Dependent Man and are attracted to him, the two of you have individual characteristics that are complementary. Therefore, his dependency is only one variable in the relationship equation. If a "caretaker" meets a man with dependency needs, a connection is probable. Some women unintentionally attract men who "need" someone to guide them though life's rough terrain (Bornstein, 1998). If you are nurturing, compassionate, and/or maternal or one of the helping personalities such as the Extravert, Intuitive, Feeling, and Perceiving personality type (ENFP in the Myers-Briggs Personality Inventory), you may unconsciously scan your environment for wounded creatures to nurse back to health. While you probably pick up a few puppies and kittens this way, you may also appropriate a Dependent Male or two. The unfortunate reality is that you may continue this frustrating course for a lifetime without ever realizing you are *choosing* needy, insecure, and manipulative men. Larry Eisenbery, author of *How Dependent Are We Really?* makes a wise suggestion, "For peace of mind, resign as general manager of the universe." Again, manipulation is not a game to Dependent Men; they firmly believe it is vital to their continued existence. They are convinced that straightforward and assertive communication will *not* accomplish their goals; this assumes they are aware that direct communication is an option. Their goal is to maneuver you surreptitiously into meeting their needs without the inconveniences inherent in a reciprocal, mutually supportive relationship.

Although they don't repay in kind, Dependent Men can be accommodating and they avoid conflict. If you desire an assertive, self-sufficient, supportive mate, look elsewhere. Nonetheless, let's not give up hope; dependent behaviors can be modified if the individual understands that his behavior threatens a valued relationship. Understanding is only the first step; he must also follow through by working persistently toward adaptive change. Change does not happen without effort, nor is it painless. If it were, the world would be populated by slim, physically fit nonsmokers.

What are the red flags that tell you a man is dependent?

Dependent Woe–Is–Me
- Avoidant
- Indecisive
- Underemployed
- Needy
- Helpless
- Fearful of criticism
- Clinging

Egotistical Woe-Is-Me
- May be successful
- Vain
- Self-centered
- Unemotional
- Demanding
- Insecure, but would not admit it
- Blames others for his misfortunes

A hostile Dependent Man will have many of the same traits. He will probably not be as concerned about his appearance, he definitely is emotional, and he may or may not be successful. Normally, his emotional outbursts limit his ability to thrive professionally. He will react with anger if he foresees potential abandonment.

Dependent Men can drain your energy. Let's observe one in our first case study.

Case Study #1: Rick and Stephanie

Stephanie, a thirty-two-year-old banking consultant, had just ended a painful relationship with an egocentric, controlling man when she met Rick. Rick, who sells shoes in an upscale store, was the opposite of her former boyfriend in many ways. She was surprised about his job. She wondered why an intelligent, well-educated man of thirty-one was selling shoes. However, Rick seemed to want to please her, he valued her opinions, and he deferred to her judgment in choosing restaurants and movies. In the beginning, she perceived Rick as a caring and giving man. Somewhere in the back of her mind, however, she wondered why he was not more assertive.

After a couple of weeks, he began to call her several times each day, at home and at work. He asked her to decide if he should trade cars, what medication to take for his cold, and how he should organize a new showcase at work. Increasingly, Stephanie felt overwhelmed by his persistent and urgent needs. For him, each decision, no matter how trivial, was a crisis. His constant need for guidance and reassurance took an inordinate amount of Stephanie's time. He was socially insecure and fearful that he would lose her.

Stephanie began to realize that she had been attracted to Rick because he was so different from her former boyfriend. She had chosen a man at one extreme (controlling) and then raced head-on to the other extreme (dependent). Perhaps she might find the middle of the continuum more comfortable. Her life was full and interesting, and she chose to wait until a more self-confident, assertive man crossed her path. Rick begged her to reconsider. He said that their relationship was perfect. He could not understand why she was not attempting to work things out. One of his statements was very telling; he insisted that he could not live without her. That was a mammoth red flag.

Stephanie knew from experience that it is always respectful to say, "Yes, you have a problem, but I have faith in you and believe that you can resolve it." If you consistently solve life's annoying little hurdles for an adult who is perfectly capable of taking responsibility, the message you send is "You are incompetent. Obviously, I must help you."

Rick's Manipulative Techniques

Blaming: He could not understand why she was not trying to work things out. If she would just try harder, everything would be fine. He did not accept any responsibility for the failure of the relationship.

Manipulating the truth: He insisted that he could not live without her. This is clearly not accurate. He may not desire to live without her, but he is certainly capable of doing so. Many manipulative types use this ploy. See it for what it is—flagrant blackmail.

Exaggeration: He must consult her before making a decision. This behavior means that he is *uncomfortable* making decisions. Clearly, he made decisions before he met Stephanie.

Exploiting emotions: Saying "I cannot live without you" is a ploy to make her feel guilty, and it is also a threat.

Case Study #2: Aaron and Tina

Aaron and Tina position themselves on opposite ends of my sofa and look expectantly at me. Tina had arranged the appointment. She told Aaron they needed help, and then she told him that if he would not attend couple's counseling, she would move out. Aaron and Tina had dated for a few weeks before moving in together; they had been living together for six months. Aaron is twenty-nine, and a tall, handsome blond man. He works in the records department of a large hospital. Tina, a petite redhead who is ten years older, is an emergency room nurse at the same hospital. When they met, they felt an immediate attraction.

Tina tells me that she is overwhelmed by Aaron's demands and moodiness. She says she understands that he lacks confidence and has difficulty making decisions. She had hoped that her love and attention would "make him whole." As an ER nurse, she is competent and giving. She is also accustomed to taking charge.

Aaron says he feels abandoned. He laments that in the beginning of their relationship, Tina was "an angel of mercy." She competently managed situations that Aaron threw in her lap. She briskly conquered anxiety-provoking tasks, and supported and reassured him. Now, according to Aaron, she is telling him to swim or drown, and he thinks their contract has been broken. He became miffed and said he couldn't understand why she had changed.

Tina is concerned that she cannot meet Aaron's expectations, raise her two children from a previous marriage, and still find the energy to be an effective professional. She is disappointed that he does not follow through when he makes promises. She feels besieged. Tears ran down her cheeks as she tells us that *she* needs someone to help her. Between bouts of weeping, she moans, "I understand how a soldier feels when she is too long on the front lines."

We discussed Aaron's insecurity and his need for constant admiration and Tina's resolve to make meaningful changes in their relationship. In the beginning, the relationship appeared compatible. Tina was in awe of Aaron (as were many nurses), and he was enthusiastically disposed to being admired. He explains that the head of his department demands that he maintain an exhausting schedule (although he works fewer hours than Tina), thus he needs Tina's help to manage his life.

Aaron is an attractive man (as you may have noticed, he has histrionic tendencies) who has always had someone to help him avoid drudgery and responsibility. His romantic relationships have been fleeting. His constant crisis demands exhaust the women in his life. He is fearful of assuming sole responsibility for himself; consequently, when a burned-out woman leaves him, he finds a new relationship. Happily for Tina, Aaron does not meet the criteria for Dependent Personality Disorder, although he has many of the traits.

Aaron's Manipulative Techniques

Passive-aggressive: He gives excuses rather than following through on his promises.

Blaming: He says Tina used to be an angel and then she changed her behavior, thereby breaking their unwritten contract. Therefore, their problems are her fault.

Whining: He explains that the head of his department demands that he maintain an exhausting schedule.

See, you should have taken responsibility: He implies that if Tina were still taking responsibility for his life, their relationship would be just fine.

Aaron asserts that he wants to save the relationship and he will do whatever it takes. According to him, this time is different; he wants to be a good mate and a dependable stepfather for her children.

Aaron says the magic words, and he appears to mean them. He does not want to be abandoned again. Unfortunately, he isn't certain what to change or where to start. Learning to relate in a more loving, assertive, and responsible manner will not be an easy task for him. Tina wants to learn to set firm boundaries and to be able to tell him when overload anxiety is creeping in. Therapy will not be brief; they accept that and commit to devoting time and attention to therapeutic change.

Other Dependent Types

Dependent individuals can be clinging and apprehensive about losing the important people in their lives. They may rush recklessly into a relationship to avoid being alone, especially if a romantic attachment has recently ended. Other than an overriding need to have a significant other, however, recklessness is not a pervasive characteristic of dependent individuals. They have a propensity to be reluctant observers of life and interpersonally accommodating. Other manipulators, such as psychopaths and antisocial types, are defined in part by their reckless, argumentative, and impulsive behavior. A Dependent Man is fearful of failure and criticism. He is unlikely to assume new responsibilities without massive doses of persuasion, support, and direction.

You may notice that he has great difficulty in making decisions. He would rather let you choose what you will do on a beautiful Saturday afternoon or which shirt he should wear. This behavior may be interpreted as thoughtful or as habitually indecisive. You will have to make that determination. If he exhibits the same behaviors in other areas of his life, such as with friends and coworkers/employers, he is leaning toward dependent. Probably, because of his low self-confidence, his career choice will allow him to avoid personal responsibility for beginning and completing tasks. He may be underemployed.

Grandiose Woe-Is-Me

Another example of a man who will rely heavily on you would be someone who simply does not want to be bothered with the minutiae of life—the Grandiose Woe-Is-Me. He may have some narcissistic characteristics: "I am too important to be bothered, and you are not." This man will demand your untiring ministrations and your boundless admiration. Remember, nothing is ever his fault. If you are the only other person present, then whatever happens is your fault. That is because, according to him, nothing untoward happens that cannot be reasonably blamed on someone else. Therefore, he will amuse you with exaggerated, entirely self-serving tales of "they done me wrong."

Although, the types of Woe-Is-Me seem to have little in common, other than making unrealistic demands on your time, there is something else. They lack self-confidence and are sensitive to criticism. The Grandiose Woe-Is-Me is better able to conceal his poor self-esteem, but he is just as needy and insecure as his timid brother, the Dependent Man. The Grandiose type feigns empathy for others, as readily as he misrepresents his achievements and veils his imperfections. After all, remember the prime directive, he is supremely significant and you are not.

Hostile Woe-Is-Me

Men who meet the criteria for Dependent Personality Disorder are normally passive—to a fault. However, some men with dependency *issues* have gone to the dark side. They are verbally, emotionally, and/or physically cruel to the women in their lives. Be assured, he would be the last person to admit he cannot survive emotionally without his mate.

If you are a successful woman, the Hostile Dependent Man will be envious and malicious. If you become annoyed with him, or critical, he feels demeaned and may become angry. He will resent anything that distracts your attention from him, including children or illness. Such men are dependent because they lack the self-confidence or skill to create a life for themselves. To maintain the illusion that they have an emotional existence, they become enmeshed with you. Their boundaries are ill defined; they perceive their mate as an extension of themselves. They may use intimidation to forestall abandonment. If you have reason to believe a man is hostile and dependent—run.

Dramatic Woe-Is-Me

This is the Dependent Man with histrionic characteristics. According to Bornstein in the *Journal of Personality Assessment*, histrionic men appear to be " . . . associated with high levels of implicit dependency needs, but low levels of self-attributed dependency needs" (1998). In other words, they have a high need to be taken care of, but they do not recognize their neediness or they won't admit it.

You are less likely to choose a histrionic male than one of the other types, because they are rare. Their self-esteem is heavily centered on their body image, physical prowess, and attractiveness. Individuals with these tendencies can be demanding, self-indulgent, and certainly dependent. Some of them can be seen at the gym—every single day. You know the ones I mean. They bore you with tedious stories about how many sets of deep knee bends they can do. They will probably dress to be noticed and to show off their best assets. If a man meets these criteria *and* has a great tan—you can reasonably guess that he has histrionic tendencies.

Naturally, they claim no responsibility for anything—the poor things.

Successful Woe-Is-Me

Not all Dependent Men are underemployed, egocentric, or emotionally sterile. Authors Gardner and Stephens (1994) explored the complexity of a talented, successful man who became emotional and potentially suicidal when his marriage dissolved: "Looking derelict, unshaven and unkempt, Albert would show up unexpectedly and plead with her to return to Boston. If she would not, he suggested, he would end his life." Yet, he could thrive in his professional environment. "He was able to persist, with a high degree of effectiveness, in the same firm for several years. Albert is not merely a manipulative man with a strong need to dominate; he had channeled these attributes—the ability to influence others and his strong competitive drive—into professionally useful skills." When you consider manipulation as an effective professional trait, many professions come to mind (i.e., law, sales, and drama).

As you see, Dependent Men come in various and sundry types. They have at least one thing in common. They are unreasonably, emotionally reliant on the women in their lives. If he has narcissistic tendencies, there may be more than one woman.

Again, Dependent Men do not want to lose their support system (you), because they sincerely believe they are unable to function successfully alone. This motivates them to modify their needy behaviors. Grandiose Dependents may not be as concerned about losing a partner; after all, there are more fish in the sea.

Starring the Dependent Man

Dependent Men are not highly valued in our society; therefore, they remain relatively obscure. Consequently, few Dependent Men are celebrities or historical figures. However, one man came to my attention; in fact, he *appears* to exemplify the Dependent Man. Some quixotic dreamers might think he is a romantic figure. Perhaps, "tragic figure" more nearly applies to his politically heretical, history-shaping personal choices. How does one describe a man who chooses to abdicate his birthright to the throne of the British Empire, at a particularly pivotal time, for the woman he loves? The Duke of Windsor made that "courageous" or "outrageous" decision, depending on one's view, in 1936. At that time, Great Britain and Germany were precariously poised on the brink of war.

According to historical speculation, the Duke of Windsor (a title he assumed after abdicating the throne) was a playboy before he met Wallis Simpson. It appears that Wallis was the stronger individual in their relationship. It was whispered in the royal halls of the empire that the duchess was also a Nazi sympathizer (from files released in 1996). When the couple made an ill-considered visit to Hitler in 1937, their allegiance and trustworthiness were open to conjecture. Many British subjects, both royal and common, chose not to trust them. Consequently, the tainted royal couple was shuttled off to the Bahamas where they could do little damage.

By choosing Mrs. Wallis Simpson, Edward VIII renounced his responsibility to guide his desperate subjects through war and reconstruction. In tolerating what many believe were Wallis' political leanings, the Duke of Windsor was branded a traitor by many of his people. Documents released by the British government in 2000 indicate that the duchess may have had affairs while dating the then–Prince Edward and after marrying him. The couple lived in exile for the rest of their lives; whether it was imposed or self-imposed is open to conjecture. The Duke and Duchess of Windsor became known for their lavish spending and for stealing the social and fashion spotlights in France and America. The king who chose an "unacceptable" mate and, consequently, political and social impotence over his royal duties died in 1972. Ever the stronger, his duchess outlived him by more than a decade.

Dealing with the Dependent Man

Most of the dependent types respond to clear, concise, and consistent messages. None of the dependent types want to change, nor do they want you to change. Woe-Is-Me Dependent types are fearful of losing relationships and facing a cold, cruel world alone. If they understand you are serious, they will probably listen.

Tell your man what you want to be different and what you are willing to do. Express this in terms of behaviors. If you simply say, "I want you to be more independent," he won't have a clue where he should start. It is more effective to say, "When I am at the office, please don't call more than twice during the day. I need every minute to finish my work before five o'clock. I really appreciate your help with this." You have asked him to change a specific behavior and told him precisely what you want. You have also expressed confidence that he will comply and your appreciation for this change. At this point, we are assuming he will cooperate. If that is not the case, you will need to choose a consequence. You have no control over him. We know that. You do have control over how you respond.

Clear Communication

What (behavior): "When I am at the office, please don't call more than twice during the day."

When: During my workday.

Why: "I need every minute to finish my work before five o'clock."

Responses

Your response is determined by his behavior.

First: If he does as you have asked, show appreciation.

Second: If he has agreed and yet does not do as you have asked, express your disappointment and talk with him about it.

Third: If he still calls you during the day, apply your consequence. Perhaps you won't have time to eat dinner together, because you are late getting home from work. This is, of course, a natural consequence. It is a logical consequence of his behavior.

In the beginning, support for his efforts, even imperfect effort, is essential. If he doesn't keep his promise, you might discuss his reasons for not changing his behavior. Life happens; he may have a reasonable explanation. However, if he continues to have "explanations," you may need to change your behavior. For example, if he does not follow through after two or three opportunities, you may say, "I had to stay late at work because I couldn't complete my assignments. I won't have time to help you with dinner tonight." He should be made aware of potential consequences. Very possibly, an undesirable consequence will influence his behavior when he is inclined to call you for the third time. Your next option, if this doesn't work, is to seek couple's counseling. Counseling will avoid turning your relationship into a battlefield of escalating negative behaviors. Naturally, if he refuses even to attempt changes, counseling would be your first option.

Egotistical Dependent Men

The illusion of perfection, maintained by projecting faults onto someone else, is a barrier to be constantly tended, mended and shored up.
↶ *Author Unknown*

Suggesting that an Egotistical Dependent Man should change is a perilous tactic fraught with gaping holes. He feels justified in getting his way; so such a request will not be received with equanimity. It is highly improbable that he will smile and say, "Sure, honey, where should I start?" If you are able to frame your suggestion in a way he can perceive as flattery, you *may* be pleasantly surprised by his willingness to cooperate. However, this will not be easily accomplished, and it puts the burden for his behavior on your already overburdened shoulders.

Also, egotistical men can be encouraged to be cooperative if your goals are tied to their goals. It would be beneficial to work with, rather than against, ego inflation. A partner who tries to deflate the ego may encounter a miffed mate.

Egotists are easily wounded and respond with extreme emotions. Their wound may engender feelings of anger or pain. If your goal is to continue the relationship, it will behoove you to enter his perception of the world and commend him. If you can convince him that the change you desire is a step toward meeting one of his goals, it increases your chance of success.

Remember, to survive we must have some egocentric tendencies. Our lives and relationships are negatively impacted when these tendencies crystallize into pervasive beliefs and then into the lens through which we perceive the world. You know your man; you are the expert who must determine if your relationship is viable. A note of caution, however: Reality-testing with an objective other is always a good idea. It is possible to enter your mate's fantasy and begin genuinely to believe he cannot cope unless the cavalry (you) arrives just in time. To avoid that trap, remember, it is disrespectful to assume your man is unable to resolve life's challenges.

The Rules: Write Them

When dealing with manipulative people, you must make clear rules and boundaries. Write them down. You both should sign them, and then keep a copy in a safe place. Dependent Men have a tendency to say, "I never promised that." If you do not have written proof, the agreement is useless. However, be prepared for an argument and a tantrum from the egotist and the hostile dependent males. If they cannot use passive-aggressive manipulation (I never promised), they will use intimidation. Therefore, even if you have a signed contract, he may not cooperate. However, it is a tool that has been successfully used many times. If possible, there should be swift and certain consequences for violating the contract. These are the rules.

1. **Be fair, reasonable, and forgiving.** Ask for cooperation in improving your relationship. Acknowledge and reward positive efforts. Many Dependent Woe-Is-Me males will probably respond to encouragement.

2. **There must be consequences for his behavior.** Some consequences are natural and they are preferable to any you can impose. For example, if he does not pay his speeding ticket because he expects you to pay it, he may lose his driver's license. Naturally, you should promptly tell him that you *will not* come to the rescue. If you say no, follow through. Otherwise, you will lose credibility and negotiation will be impossible.

3. **Choose your battles carefully.** Begin with one important issue and resolve it before attempting another major advance. Choose the issue that annoys you the most. This

issue should also be the one that creates the most distress in your relationship. After it is resolved, you are ready to go to the next level. Or, you may decide to begin with the issue that is most amendable to change.

Again, egotists and Hostile Dependent Men will probably not play fairly, and they will retaliate for perceived impertinent behavior. The best predictor of his future behavior is his past behavior. Choose your strategy accordingly.

4. **Don't be swayed by excuses.** When he blames you, he gives up his power to change. Excuses are meant to absolve a person of responsibility and to help him or her evade consequences. If your partner says, "I know that I promised to take our clothes to the cleaners, but I overslept," the bottom line is "I didn't take our clothes to the cleaners." That is the message you can effectively address. Don't get lost in his forest of excuses.

5. **Avoid the blame game.** Dependent Men are terrified of making a mistake; therefore, it is more comfortable—in fact, it is essential—for you to be at fault. Dependent Men believe you "must" take care of them, so if they make a mistake you "should" have made certain it would not happen. They are mistaken. Hostile types may know they are wrong, but they believe they can distract your attention from their shortcomings. I hope they are mistaken.

6. **There is strength in numbers.** Hang on to your friends; they will help you stay focused. Friends will be happy to tell you when you are being misled or distracted.

The Bottom Line

You love him and you have valiantly attempted to explain your concerns and ask for help in making positive changes. The types in this chapter, with the possible exception of the Dependent

Man, are resistant to change. Sometimes, despite your best efforts, weeds crowd out your roses and Roundup is the only solution. A good gardener knows when to spray. You deserve roses.

Now 'tis the spring, and weeds are shallow-rooted.
Suffer them now, and they'll o'ergrow the garden
And choke the herbs for want of husbandry.
William Shakespeare

The Dependent Man Test

Do you have a Dependent Man? Take the test.

1. Does he blame you for his mistakes?
   Yes ○   No ○

2. Does he avoid the words "I am sorry" like the Black Death?
   Yes ○   No ○

3. Is he self-involved?
   Yes ○   No ○

4. Is he extremely sensitive to criticism?
   Yes ○   No ○

5. Does your relationship sometimes feel as if it were parent to child?
   Yes ○   No ○

6. Does he believe he is entitled to special treatment?
   Yes ○   No ○

7. Does he get angry if you express your honest opinion (if it does not agree with his)?
   Yes ○   No ○

8. Does he make excuses rather than produce results?
Yes ○   No ○

9. Does he expect you to carry a disproportionate part of family responsibilities?
Yes ○   No ○

10. Has he had an unusual number of romantic relationships?
Yes ○   No ○

11. Does he use intimidation to manipulate you?
Yes ○   No ○

12. Are you beginning to think he is crabgrass?
Yes ○   No ○

13. Does he have periods of depression?
Yes ○   No ○

14. Is he frequently disgruntled?
Yes ○   No ○

15. Does he appear to believe that his time is more important than yours?
Yes ○   No ○

16. Does he complain that others are out to get him?
Yes ○   No ○

17. Is he vengeful?
Yes ○   No ○

18. Does he frequently make promises he does not keep?
Yes ○   No ○

19. Do minor inconveniences distress him?
Yes ○   No ○

20. Does he avoid emotional intimacy, preferring adoration?
     Yes ○   No ○

21. Is he frequently in crisis?
     Yes ○   No ○

22. Does he expect you to save him?
     Yes ○   No ○

Scoring the Test

Give yourself one point for each yes answer.

Scores 1 to 9

Congratulations! Yes, there are a few weeds in your garden; however, they will probably respond to a light hand. The killer sprays and sharp hoe should be reserved for the next two groups. Of course, some of the questions concern indicators that are quite serious in and of themselves. The indicators in numbers 10 and 11 are probably the most troublesome for mates.

The suggestions in this chapter may be all you need to transform your relationship. However, couple's counseling is always an option.

Scores 10 to 16

If your man is in this category, your relationship has several significant issues. The good news is, you know there's a problem and you know its severity. Your next step is the most important. Sit down with a nice cup of rich, fragrant coffee and make a list of your options. It might read something like this:

1. Take care of myself.
   a. Eat healthful foods.
   b. Get adequate exercise.
   c. Spend time with people who make me feel good.
   d. Take time to relax and regroup each day.
2. Specific behaviors I want to target for change (i.e., He doesn't listen when I talk to him).
3. My strategy for each behavior:
   a. Talk to him about "not listening."
   b. Tell him how it affects our relationship and me.
   c. Give him reasons it would be in his interest to change.
   d. Make a contract with him about change.
   e. Get the phone number of a good couple's therapist.
4. Do reality-testing with a friend.

Always start any relationship strategy with a plan for taking care of *you* first. Attempting to make alterations in a relationship can be stressful; you need to feel your strongest.

Remember, the more severe his symptomatology is, the more difficult it will be to gain his cooperation.

Scores 17 to 22

You are struggling in this relationship. Your stress level is probably extremely high. Look at the strategies for taking care of yourself in the previous section.

When symptoms reach this level, a good couple's counselor is my first choice. If your mate is egocentric, he can probably delude the therapist. Remain calm and consistent. The counselor will soon learn who is being straightforward and sincere. No matter which type he is, he will attempt to sway the counselor. Fortunately, we counselors are accustomed to that ploy. The road ahead will probably be bumpy, so hang in there.

How do you know when it is time to say, "I have done all I can do. I can do no more"? If he continues to resist cooperation or employs intimidation, you may have reached the point of diminishing return.

Conclusion

As in all relationships, there are advantages and disadvantages in choosing a dependent mate. Dependent Men are likely to be attentive and agreeable. They value your opinion and frequently request your advice. When they are not in crisis, they can be quite companionable. Regretfully, they are often in crisis and you can be caught up in their anxiety. They can and will cooperate with you if you are straightforward and ask for their cooperation, especially if they know you are serious about the consequences. They value their relationship with you, partly because they abhor the very notion of being left to fend for themselves.

If your Dependent Man has few symptoms or if they are slight, the comprehensive contract for change should do the job. If his symptoms are numerous or severe, begin to look for a good counselor.

If you would like a drastic change from the Dependent Man, you have come to the right place. We are about to meet the Antisocial. He is more exciting, charming, and fun loving. He also has more self-confidence and is secure in his masculinity. These are not his only delusions. The world he has built for himself is alien to the one in which we live. In his world, you strike first, con your way through life, sneer at the idea of love, and seize what you want. Nothing is as it seems when you have an Antisocial in your life. He will keep only one promise; when he tells you life with him will never be boring, believe him.

CHAPTER 6

Exciting Risk-Takers and
Full-Blown Antisocials

Living at risk is jumping off the cliff and building your wings on the way down.
ᕦ *Ray Bradbury*

RISK-TAKERS AND ANTISOCIALS ARE FUN. It is easy to become entranced by them. They are the daring, high-maintenance sports cars of the manipulators. Their bold behaviors especially appeal to certain women. Are you one of those women? Do you enjoy the buzz from a hefty rush of adrenaline? Do you just adore the exhilarating roar of a red Corvette? Do you feel a melancholy yen to frolic with frightening and thrilling exotic animals such as lions, tigers, and bears? Would you like to dive into a gurgling public fountain, feel the air on your tingling, bare skin, and splash among the superfluous pennies? Do you daydream about distant enchanting lands bejeweled with emerald palms, shimmering sand crystals, and sapphire-tinted water?

Is your life filled with rewarding events and stimulating conversations? Or, do you end each dreary day with a huge sigh, relieved that it has finally ended? Are you nurturing and caring? Do your friends run to you when they need a shoulder to cry on?

Whether you are on an estrogen/testosterone/adrenaline overload or you are a Mother Walton type, you may be a likely target for an Exciting Risk-Taker (Antisocial or Antisocial wannabe). However, these manipulative men are more likely to take advantage of the motherly type, because the former will probably hold her own quite well. These bad boy, lawless adventurers have a sixth sense for recognizing women who are caretakers (i.e., nurses, therapists, social workers). They are experts at telling us exactly what we want to hear and dangling excitement before our dazzled eyes. They can create the reality we have dreamed about on many a lackluster night. They can accurately read our vulnerabilities in one brief conversation. Exciting Risk-Takers (ERT) instinctively know how to exploit our vulnerabilities to gain an advantage and to control us.

Some thrill-seeking women understand this deceitful type and choose to enjoy the journey. It can be an exhilarating, though brief ride, if you don't mind the mammoth potholes. Sadly, for this type and his lady of the moment, the speed bumps typically wear a badge and carry a weapon. Exciting Risk-Takers have an alarming tendency to ignore laws, such as driving violations, drug- and alcohol-related issues, physical aggression, and other annoying (inconvenient to obey) legal restrictions. They are superficially charming, boyish bullies and conmen.

Research has linked bullying with violent and criminal behavior later in life, as well as with emotional, psychological, and social problems. A federally funded study published in 2004 indicated that bullies and their victims had more health problems and poorer emotional and social adjustment than their peers (*www.MontereyHerald.com*, August 27, 2005). Do Antisocials begin taking advantage of others at an early age? It appears that they do.

Do you have a Risk-Taker or Antisocial in your life? Would you recognize him? If not, let's remedy that problem.

Criteria for Antisocials and Exciting Risk-Takers

It is unlikely that any one man will have all of these characteristics, but it is not impossible.

- Deceptive
- Lawless
- Self-centered
- Adrenaline junky
- Frequent substance abuser
- Cannot or will not control anger
- Physically and verbally aggressive
- Unable to connect emotionally with others
- Shallow
- Lacks the capacity to love (as we understand love)
- Irresponsible (bills not paid, promises not kept)
- Opportunistic
- Superficially charming
- Exciting
- Primitively perceptive

Our task in recognizing this type of manipulative man is complicated by their almost mystic ability to cloak negative traits at the beginning of a relationship. If you have had a relationship with one, you are aware of their shape-shifting talent. You can meet a sweet Dr. Jekyll and wake up with an obnoxious Mr. Hyde. Or even worse, Mr. Hyde has disappeared with your BMW, your American Express card, and the rainy-day cash that was hidden in the cookie jar (as well as all of your Fig Newtons).

In which case, the rainy day you were saving for has arrived. Why don't we learn more about Exciting Risk-Takers from Nadine?

Case Study #1: Jarrod and Nadine

Nadine thought she had met Mr. Right when Jarrod slithered into her life. His superficial charm and self-confidence made her spine tingle with excitement. She told friends, "I have never met another man like Jarrod. He is just unique, really wonderful!" They have been dating for a short while, and Nadine tries to contact Jarrod after he missed a lunch date. This is their dialogue, or rather her side of a one-way conversation.

Nadine calls Jarrod and reaches his answering machine—2:00 P.M.: Jarrod, are you okay? I have not heard from you in a couple of days. I was certain that you said (when I lent you the money for your brother's hospital bill) to meet you today for lunch. I waited at our café for over an hour. I suppose I misunderstood the time or place. Please call me when you come in. I love you.

Nadine calls Jarrod and reaches his answering machine—4:00 P.M.: Hello, Jarrod ... I guess I've missed you again. I am afraid that you've re-injured your leg. It was so brave of you to save that child from drowning. Call me. I am worried.

Nadine calls Jarrod and reaches his answering machine—11:00 P.M.: I just don't know what to think. I am so worried. Did the FBI ask for your help again? Still, I wish you had called. You swore I am your soul mate and the most beautiful woman in the world, but I guess I still wonder ... I am being silly ... never mind ... I love you.

Nadine calls Jarrod and reaches his answering machine—4:00 A.M.: I am frightened now. I pray you have not been in an accident. I couldn't stand losing you. Call me as soon as you get this message. Please.

Do you think that Nadine will hear from Jarrod (or whatever his real name is)? I think it is highly improbable, unless another sibling has an unpaid hospital bill. Jarrod sees Nadine as a free source of supplies. The supplies could be sex, money, drugs (many Antisocials and Risk-Takers have addictions), a car, room and board, or whatever Jarrod desires at the moment.

Let's look at Jarrod's manipulative techniques.

JARROD'S MANIPULATIVE TECHNIQUES

False intimacy: "*You swore that we were soul mates.*" This statement tells us that Jarrod implied an intimate connection when he was a virtual stranger. Yes, one can fall in love in under eight minutes according to some recent studies. However, Jarrod is incapable of falling in love.

Manipulating the truth: Do you believe that Jarrod has a brother with hospital bills, works with the FBI, or saved a child from drowning? I would rather doubt it. These men are talented prevaricators, probably in the same esteemed category as psychopaths.

Charming and complimentary: His statement that Nadine is {you are} "the most beautiful woman" does not ring true considering his other larger-than-life embellishments. However, his compliments certainly got Nadine's attention.

Deception is the tool most often used by Exciting Risk-Takers to manipulate their victims. If they were to state clearly, "I am incapable of loving. I will take whatever I want without remorse. You cannot trust anything I say, because I am a pathological liar. Now, may I borrow your car?" it probably would not work as well for them.

A few years ago, a charming ERT confessed that merely thinking about how much he loved his daughters overwhelmed him with unendurable emotions. His fatherly devotion brought tears to my eyes, until I remembered he was ill equipped to understand, much less feel, love.

Case Study #2: Juan and Lilly

Lilly called to make the appointment. She sounded as if she were trying desperately to control her emotions. She asked for couple's counseling and the first available appointment.

Lilly arrived for the appointment alone. This is what she told me: "Dr. McCoy, I don't know where to start. I know you will think I am a silly middle-aged (Lilly is forty-eight) woman. Please believe me. I have never been frivolous or romantic. I am the head librarian for the university here. I have a master's degree and I scored in the top 5 percent of my class."

"I never planned to marry. My mother said I was a Plain Jane and I suppose she was right. Mother was a beautiful woman and I think she was ashamed of me. She said I had better prepare myself to make a living, because men would never flock to me. I prepared to make a living and I have been working for the university since I graduated.

"I thought that I was content with my life until I met Juan. It was October 31 and I was attending the university's Halloween dance with my friend Joyce. As usual, we helped with refreshments and complained about the administration with the other staff.

"I suddenly felt that someone was watching me. I looked up and into the beautiful eyes of a tall, handsome stranger. My throat constricted and I didn't think I would be able to speak. He asked me if I wanted to dance. I was dumbfounded—absolutely shocked. Men don't ask me to dance, especially not handsome men. He did not wait for my answer; he took my hand and led me to the dance floor. I still could not speak. He chatted easily. Juan is so self-confident. Juan said I was the woman he had been waiting for all of his life. He told me had had beautiful dreams in which he saw my face, so he recognized me right away. He called me the 'woman of his dreams.' I truly felt as if I was in a dream.

"I assumed that my dream would end with the dance. Nevertheless, he asked for my phone number and called me. I have never been so shocked. We were together every night. After a week, he asked me to marry him. I have a large, old house and make a generous salary, so money was not an issue. He said that he was an artist trying to get established in this area. Though I must admit that I was concerned about our age difference; at twenty-eight, he is younger than I. He moved in with me a few days after we met and it was heaven at first. I didn't mind loaning money to him so he could market his paintings and pay the down payment on a car.

"Then he became sullen and quiet. Everything I said or did made him angry or irritable. He told me to leave him alone. I was heartbroken. That's when I made the counseling appointment.

"His sullen mood wasn't the worst of it. A week ago, a police officer came to my door and asked for Juan. When Juan came in, the officer put handcuffs on him and took him away. I begged Juan and the officer to tell me what was happening. I just knew it was a crazy mistake. Why would Juan be under arrest? The officer told me that Juan was wanted for fraud, embezzlement, and theft. I felt as if I had been kicked in the stomach. Then I knew. It hit me like a ton of bricks. I had been a silly fool.

"To tell you the truth, Dr. McCoy, I don't think Juan is an artist. I think everything he said was a lie. Now I feel dimwitted and naive. I gave thousands of dollars to him and I don't think

I'll get any of it back. What will people think of me? I am so depressed. Can you help me?"

Lilly was not a fool. Juan was a very competent conman. Some of Juan's manipulative behaviors are listed here:

JUAN'S MANIPULATIVE TECHNIQUES

Creating a fantasy: He told Lilly that she was the "woman of his dreams." He uttered pretty words that made her feel like Cinderella at the ball. Lilly felt attractive and desirable. She was no longer a Plain Jane; an attractive man wanted her. Her mother was wrong. Juan gave Lilly the fantasy in which she could live happily ever after.

Charming and complimentary: Juan told Lilly what she wanted to hear.

Manipulating the truth: "He said he was an artist trying to get established in this area." Perhaps, he believed that artists aren't expected to be gainfully employed. Artist? I don't think so.

False intimacy: Lilly was the "woman of his dreams." Even before they met, according to Juan, they were destined to be a couple.

Are men who share characteristics with Juan rare? I am afraid not, and they may increase in number. Neil Strauss' book, *The Game,* which debuted in September, reveals a "series of psychological tricks guaranteed to work (seduce women), regardless of wealth or looks. It will delight saloon bar Casanovas everywhere" (Johnson, *Independent on Line,* August 2005). It is supposed to work "using the kind of magician's psychology normally associated with master mentalist Derren Brown, and other techniques such as neuro-linguistic programming, they claim no woman is off-limits." Naturally, women who have heard about the book have had a strong reaction. Germaine Greer, author of *The Female Eunuch*, decries the use of pseudo-psychological gimmicks to ensnare women. Ms. Greer says, "I've always told young women who think they are looking for Mr. Right that they are really searching for Mr. Wrong, because that is who the exciting, charismatic charmer normally turns out to be. It's profoundly destructive behavior." It appears that the wolves may soon outnumber the sheep.

Starring the Antisocial

Interestingly, psychopaths tend to hunt alone, whereas Antisocials often seek the company of their fellows. Thus, biker gangs, the Mafia, prison gangs, and adolescent gangs proliferate. It is not unusual for mob gangsters to knock off rival mob gangsters. In fact, it is a commonplace occupational hazard. Antisocials tend to be paranoid because they believe that everyone thinks as they think. Therefore, their motto is "I must eliminate you before you have the opportunity to kill me. Pity, but life goes on." Consequently, they sleep with one eye open, ever watchful, listening for a knock at their door.

Michael Corleone of *Godfather* fame is the classic sociopath or remorseless miscreant. Michael was born into the Corleone crime family in the 1930s. To be just, I will leave you to speculate about plausible personality differences had he been born into the Walton family. As the movie develops, Michael responds to a series of criminal events. He gradually progresses from a likeable young soldier to a coldhearted, ostensibly dissociated killer.

Early in the movie, Michael tells Kay, his soon-to-be second wife, that he loves and needs her. She has not seen him in two years and is unaware of his moral regression. In the last scene of the *Godfather*, Kay implores Michael to tell her he did not order his brother-in-law's death. Michael warns her not to question him about his business (an Antisocial can righteously believe that murder is a rational business decision). He then relinquishes and graciously agrees to answer *one* business question. Michael looks into Kay's eyes and with extraordinary sincerity lies through his teeth. If you have seen the movie, you may have noticed that the Corleones', husband and wife, collude in this blatant deception. Kay could not hear the truth and Michael would not speak it. Antisocials are successful because many individuals would rather be deceived than hear a painful truth, especially if that truth demands an action. Such was the case with Kay Corleone.

Is your mate an Exciting Risk-Taker? Here is your opportunity to find out.

Dealing with the Antisocial

If you enjoy the excitement of an Antisocial and want to save your relationship, a few behavior changes may be all that is necessary. Keep in mind that they are not normally attracted to long-term commitments. They are drawn to the new and exhilarating. Domestic bliss is not their cup of tea.

Decide what you need from him. It will not be as easy as sitting down and discussing your relationship with him. One, he may make promises he will not keep. Two, he may get angry and stomp out of the room. In either case, you have not accomplished anything.

Here is what you can do to encourage cooperation. He will follow your lead or not.

1. **Be fair, reasonable, and forgiving.** If you see positive behavior changes, tell him how important they are to you. Thank him for being cooperative. Do not thank him for words; words without behavior changes are useless. In the beginning, expect him to make mistakes. Change is not easy. Like the psychopath, his question will probably be "What's in it for me?"

2. **There must be consequences for his behavior.** He has spent his entire life trying to avoid consequences. He will not embrace them now. He may turn nasty when you mention the *C*-word. You can allow him to accept consequences by not attempting to bail him out of trouble. For example, if he refuses to go to work, don't call his boss and make excuses. Listening to his boss grumble is a consequence of not going to work.

   If you apply consequences, be careful it does not put you in a perilous situation. Even therapists find people with antisocial traits tricky.

   Dr. David Black explains why Antisocials and their ilk are challenging, "Because antisocials tend to blame others, have a low tolerance for frustration, are impulsive and rarely form trusting relationships, working with these individuals is difficult. People with antisocial personality disorder (ASP) often lack the motivation to improve and are notoriously poor self-observers. They simply do not see themselves as others do."

3. **Don't be swayed by excuses.** They are experts at avoiding, denying, blaming, and excusing. Don't be taken in by constant excuses. True, even Exciting Risk-Takers occasionally have a flat tire or a dead phone battery. You know your

mate and can probably judge which excuses are genuine. If he says, "I will pick you up at work at five," there should be a verifiable reason for not picking you up until six. If it happens frequently, logic tells us that no one's luck is that consistently bad.

Going to therapy with your Exciting Risk-Taker may be beneficial. The counseling may help your mate understand how his behavior impacts you, and it will discourage his use of excuses to manipulate the therapist. Therapists who specialize in family counseling may help address the "antisocial person's trouble maintaining an enduring attachment to his spouse or partner, his inability to be an effective parent, problems with honesty and responsibility, and the anger and hostility that can lead to domestic violence (Black, Psych Central, 2003).

4. **Be consistent.** These types are virtually devoid of consistency and structure. If you are consistent and do not allow him to manipulate you, your mate will learn that he cannot play his game with you. He may begin to take you and what you say seriously. That does not necessarily mean you will make any progress toward change. You must understand the Exciting Risk-Takers and Antisocials. They are known most for their absolute lack of remorse. They have "almost stereotypical disregard for others; fail to conform in all aspects, especially lawful behavior; are deceitful, impulsive" (Della Santa-Percy, Russell 2002, 2004), and are "irritable, aggressive and reckless . . . " (Adams, 2000). In addition, they are inconsistent in work situations, do not honor obligations, and can "rationalize their taking from, or harming of, others" (Adams, 2000).

If you are successful in overcoming all of the beliefs and behaviors that characterize this type, then you will make progress toward a mutually satisfying relationship. I am afraid that is improbable. However, consistency on your part will add the structure you need to survive emotionally.

5. **Choose your battles carefully.** In addition to consistency, you will also need patience. Choosing one or two battles rather than focusing on each transgression will require supreme patience. The battles you choose should meet at least two criteria. One, the fight should be something you can win. Two, the battle should be near and dear to your heart. Launching a grand attack to get the trash taken out on Fridays is not worth your blood, sweat, and tears.

    Make a list of everything you would like to be different in the order of importance. Scratch off the ones you cannot win. The top two left on the list will probably be your best bets.

    Before you do battle with an Exciting Risk-Taker, be certain that you understand their Geneva Convention rules of war. They are high-conflict personalities. Social worker and attorney William Eddy, author of *High Conflict Personalities*, has worked with these difficult individuals for more than thirty years.

    He says that the most "striking characteristic of high conflict personalities is—their actions are so self-sabotaging and out of proportion with external events that they seem beyond comprehension." Interestingly, those with personality disorders or maladaptive personality traits tend to be those who rely more heavily on others to help them reach their goals. Mr. Eddy has seen the following pattern in court over the years.

    Unfortunately, many Persuasive Blamers have developed highly effective skills in short-term emotional persuasion, including: charm, heightened emotions, and the ability to persuade others that they are the victims—even when they are the perpetrator.

Conflict with an Exciting Risk-Taker or other high-conflict personality type will be unpleasant and long term. Be prepared to turn to your support system. You may feel very alone.

6. **Avoid the blame game.** He will blame you or someone for everything that happens. He will not accept blame unless it is part of his plan to control you. The following tips may help you relate constructively:

- Don't be swayed by charm.
- Ask for evidence when in doubt.
- Use your logic and intellect.
- Don't expect him to change his blaming behavior (it has worked for him).
- Don't try to save him (he is perfectly happy with himself).
- If you feel fearful, listen to your instinct.
- Keep firm boundaries (understand your responsibility and where it ends).
- Demand the truth even when it is painful to hear.

To keep your sanity, write everything down and reality-test with friends. Remember, you do not have to defend yourself from blame, simply ignore it. If you defend yourself each time he blames you, you will never resolve any issue. Blaming is a game with a goal of creating confusion and distraction; don't play.

7. **There is strength in numbers.** He is an expert at using advocates. Your support system will be especially important to you in this relationship. Your friends and family will help penetrate the dense emotional fog generated by his manipulative tactics. Listen to your friends, they are removed from his influence (we hope) and will have a more objective perspective.

Consider seeing a therapist to help you examine your options. Many studies have strongly suggested that an adequate support system is essential for optimal physical and emotional health. Keep in touch by regularly e-mailing, calling, and going out with your friends and family.

Now you are armed with knowledge about your Risk-Taker and you can make informed decisions. Understanding what he is doing and why he is doing it magically transforms you into a worthy challenger. Remember the basics of risk-taker survival:

- Realize his words are just so much hot air; behaviors are the genuine evidence of change.
- You are not going crazy. He does outlandish things.
- You have the same power and choice he has: you can leave the relationship, change it, or accept it as it is.
- Have faith in your strength, and your ability to call on it when it is needed.

The Bottom Line

You may be approaching the point where you decide if your mate or lover is bringing anything of value into your life. What is he getting in return? If you believe you can change him into the lovable human being who lies buried beneath that obnoxious exterior (where the real Antisocial is revealed), please take a deep breath and think again. That is who he is; the sweet, wounded little boy is the mask. Remember, his mask is his stock-in–trade; without it, he would be just another malcontent loser.

He is perfectly capable of taking care of himself; it is his primary directive. Now, please take a moment to consider how you will take care of yourself.

The Exciting Risk-Taker Test

Is your man an Exciting Risk-Taker? Take the test.

1. Does he have a criminal record?
    Yes ○   No ○

2. Did he get in trouble with authority before age fifteen?
    Yes ○   No ○

3. Has he been caught telling lies?
    Yes ○   No ○

4. Does he disregard your rights and concerns?
    Yes ○   No ○

5. Has he been involved in physical aggression?
    Yes ○   No ○

6. Is he verbally aggressive?
    Yes ○   No ○

7. Does he have a spotty employment record?
    Yes ○   No ○

8. Does he avoid paying his bills?
    Yes ○   No ○

9. Does he associate with individuals with criminal records?
    Yes ○   No ○

10. Is he self-centered?
    Yes ○   No ○

11. Does he frequently display uncontrolled anger?
    Yes ○   No ○

12. Does he frequently break promises?
    Yes ○   No ○

Scoring the Test

Give one point for each yes answer.

Scores 0 to 4

If your score was 0, congratulations—your mate is not an Exciting Risk-Taker. If it was higher than 1, you may have reason for concern. Questions 1, 4, and 5 are particularly indicative of a male predator. None of the questions are neutral. If he has a score of 4, you are in a relationship with someone who could be problematic. Please do some reality-testing with friends and family.

Scores 5 to 8

These scores are moderately high, and because of the nature of the questions, they indicate a serious problem. Your mate may not qualify for the diagnosis of Antisocial, but it appears that he may be a wannabe. The characteristics he has create serious issues for you and for him. Now may be a good time to sit back, have a nice cup of tea, and consider where you are and where this relationship is taking you. Yes, I know these men can be heartbreakingly charming and it is easy to love them. Before you follow your heart, please talk to your family and friends, show them the test, and listen to them.

Scores 8 or higher

Your mate may qualify for the diagnosis of Antisocial, or he may simply have a number of behavioral issues. Either way, this relationship will be emotionally and psychologically challenging. I sincerely wish I had better news for you. Sometimes when the other person is unable to meet us halfway, the only thing we can do is save ourselves. Antisocial Personality Disorder is, as the name implies, a personality disorder and as such is very resistant to change. Read everything you can find on the disorder and then talk to your friends and family. I wish you luck.

If your guy's score on the test was very low, positive changes may be possible. You probably understand him and his limitations better after reading this chapter. You are aware that he is unlikely ever to be warm and fuzzy.

Conclusion

You may know an Antisocial or Exciting Risk-Taker. If you do, you now recognize him for what he is. The mist is clearing and your knowledge is increasing. You know he is charming, thrilling, and one step ahead of the local law enforcement agency. I can think of some I have met who are eagerly sought by multiple jurisdictions. It gives a person a warm feeling to be wanted. The Antisocial's excitement begins to tarnish when we understand the dangers involved. It is also very possible that he has an addiction. It could be illegal drugs, alcohol, or sex. His addiction may even be gambling; the evidence is accumulating.

We will now leave the ever-challenging Antisocial to explore the charismatic and charmingly deceptive Womanizer and Player. Of course, the Womanizer can also be an Antisocial because they, too, are known for changing partners with regularity. Yes, that fact also made me noticeably pale. The Womanizer or Player will probably not end his life in prison. The same cannot be said for the Antisocial. The Player enjoys women and, in his own way, esteems them, even when he is being patently insincere. The Womanizer and Antisocial have their own egocentric agendas, which are definitely not in the woman's best interest, nor do they esteem her. Meet the Womanizer and Player.

CHAPTER 7

The
Womanizer

I rather like my reputation, actually, that of a spoiled genius from the Welsh gutter, a drunk, a womanizer; it's rather an attractive image.
✍ *Richard Burton*

ARE YOU CONCERNED that your man may be a Womanizer? Let's talk about terms for a minute. A Womanizer enjoys conquering and hurting women. In spite of appearances, even considering their philandering behavior, they don't like or respect women. On the other hand, Players strive to prove that they are okay. Each woman conquered is a stepping stone to that elusive place they hope is secreted away somewhere inside of them that says, "You have finally proven that you are worthy. Now, you can cease woman-hopping and enjoy your new self-confidence. Congratulations." Unfortunately, that place doesn't exist and there will never be enough women to create it. Women genuinely like Players. Even when we are aware that the player is not, and is not likely to become, faithful, we are still drawn to him. However, Womanizers are unlikely to leave many female fans in their wake.

King Henry VIII (1491–1547) was the supreme Renaissance Womanizer. He continued his womanizing reign until he was too ill to track and overpower women. His sixth wife, Catherine Parr, was also his last wife, primarily because she had the good fortune to become his widow. King Henry was a Womanizer, rather than a Player, due to his nasty habit of having tiresome wives beheaded.

A couple of hundred years ago, Womanizers and Players were called "men of high gallantry." In other words, this pleasant little euphemism meant that "boys will be boys." The label attached to women who enjoyed a variety of men (or were thought to) was not quite so pleasant. Men who fall into these categories are frequently unable or unwilling to change. The thrill of the pursuit is simply too addictive to abandon.

Do you have a Player or a Womanizer in your life? Much like the Psychopath and Antisocial, they are charming and attractive. They are concerned about their appearance, possibly quite vain, and socially at ease. They, too, must be able to read a woman's personality with very little exposure to her. They must understand what she wants from a man and give it to her—temporarily. Remember, these men do not value long-term relationships. They are often shallow and unable to establish and maintain an emotionally intimate relationship with a woman. The next time you attend a party, watch the good looking, self-confident, well-dressed man working the room. You will notice he is talking to the loveliest women, and he is standing close (within their space), peering into their eyes. The women are speaking in low voices and laughing. Very possibly, you have just spotted a Womanizer or a Player.

Peggy Vaughan, author of *The Monogamy Myth*, estimates that 60 percent of husbands will have an affair at some point in their marriage. This, of course, does not include the men who are marathon daters and are not married. No doubt, the online dating services are littered with them. For them, numbers matter; home and hearth do not.

Women are naturally attracted to the bad-boy image of the Womanizer and Player. We may not break the rules, but we find excitement in dating the man who creates and follows his own set of laws. We can vicariously enjoy a walk on the wild side. Remember what Mom said about playing with fire? It can be exhilarating knowing that we can lose our footing and fall at any moment, as we desperately balance on the edge of the inferno. Beware, flames scorch and carry a price tag.

One study suggests that attractive men are better able to successfully pursue frequent, fleeting sexual relationships with multiple partners (Gangestad and Simpson, 1990, 47). Logically, if a handsome, desirable man sweeps you off your feet, you are probably not his first conquest. We can also assume you will not be his last.

Are you being manipulated by a Womanizer or a Player? Perhaps you have good reason to be suspicious. Although behaviors will vary from individual to individual, we can make some generalizations. Our focus is on serial affairs of the heart or more probably the libido. This behavior normally extends for a long period. It may begin in young manhood and can extend into geezerhood.

A man can have an affair or pursue more than one relationship without being a Womanizer or a Player. Individuals can "tumble" into rival relationships that are unintentional and uncharacteristic of them. This does not happen repeatedly, no matter what he says.

Criteria for the Womanizer and the Player

There are no official criteria for the Womanizer or Player, because they are not considered pathological disorders. He may also have a *DSM-IV-TR* personality disorder; he definitely has some characteristics of the Antisocial, Psychopath, and/or Narcissist. Without official criteria, we will focus on the characteristics normally associated with the Womanizer or Player as defined by our society.

I am going to list them separately because there are a few significant differences.

The Player
- Attractive and well dressed
- Well dressed
- Smooth
- Frequently well educated
- Intelligent
- Interesting
- Persuasive
- Insecure (you probably will not see the insecurity)
- Convincing liar
- Short-term intimate relationships
- Irresponsible in intimate relationships
- Professional-quality flirt
- Pleasant, easygoing manner
- Likes and enjoys the company of women

Womanizer
The criteria for the Womanizer will be the same as for the Player with the exception of the last two. Instead, the Womanizer will exhibit the following criteria:

- Does not like or respect women
- Can be temperamental and cruel
- May take advantage of women for gain

The Womanizer is reminiscent of the old-fashioned gigolo. However, taking money from the women he seduces is not a criterion for Womanizer status.

Women are no more than a notch on their gun or the unknowing prey of such men. Have you felt hunted? Let's take a look at our first couple, Derrick and Megan.

Case Study #1: Derrick and Megan

Derrick is tall, blond, and devastatingly charming. He is a sports announcer for a popular radio station in a major city. Megan met Derrick at a Save the Whales function. She saw him standing across the room and could not resist looking his way every few minutes. He returned her glance and added a brilliant smile. That was all it took; she was hooked.

They began to date and after a couple of whirlwind weeks, Derrick started making excuses for not calling her and breaking dates with short notice. He said he had to work late or he had to attend a meeting. He constantly complained that he was overworked. Whenever Megan asked questions about his absences, he accused her of trying to smother him. Afraid that she would push him away, she resisted asking questions—for a while.

After these absences, Derrick would call Megan and act as if nothing had happened. Then the absences would start again.

After enduring this for a few weeks, Megan decided to chance incurring his wrath and called him. A young female voice answered the phone. Surprised, Megan hung up. At first, she thought she had dialed the wrong number. She checked the number and it was correct. She called back and Derrick answered. He was angry and loudly accused her of spying on him. She hung up feeling humiliated and needy.

When Derrick called the next day, he said his niece had been visiting him and he was very apologetic about losing his temper. Megan began to wonder if she were losing her mind, or perhaps, she hoped, his behavior really was peculiar.

Derrick manipulated Megan using the following techniques:

Derrick's Manipulative Techniques

Blaming: I am okay; you are smothering me and spying. Derrick cannot be the problem—because, obviously Megan is the problem.

Shrew: The previous statement also carries the message that Megan's expectations are unreasonable.

Exaggeration and lying: Poor Derrick is so overworked he does not have time to call or e-mail Megan. His niece was visiting with him.

Exploiting negative beliefs: Megan began to doubt her sanity. He constantly reassured her that, indeed, she was unbalanced.

Exploiting emotions and intimidating: Megan was afraid of Derrick's anger; therefore, she resisted asking for what she needed from him and setting firm limits. Wouldn't it be interesting if a female Psychopath met a Womanizer?

Some Womanizers have a primary relationship that they cling to while enjoying other relations on the side. Perhaps they do this because they can reasonably explain to other women who become possessive that "I am sorry, but I am married and the shrew won't allow me to leave the marriage because . . . ."

Or they may stay because they need the appearance of a stable relationship to further their career. Politicians would fall into this category.

Let's look at our next couple, Allen and Darlene.

Case Study #2: Allen and Darlene

Allen called to make an appointment for marriage counseling. He sounded desperate and insisted on an appointment that afternoon. I was booked, so he had to wait a few days. His tone clearly expressed his displeasure. I soon formed the impression that he was accustomed to getting what he wanted.

Allen and his wife, Darlene, were a few minutes late for their appointment. His wife apologized. He was late meeting her, so they couldn't arrive on time. I wondered if Allen was using passive-aggressive manipulation to "punish" me because his appointment was not scheduled on demand. I also wondered if he used passive-aggressive behavior to manipulate other people.

Darlene was in tears for most of the session. She said she had tried everything and felt as if she were losing her mind. Allen sat there the epitome of calmness and reasonableness. His facial express said, "See what I have to endure from this woman."

Darlene brought out a small black notebook and began to recite the names of women with whom Allen had been involved. She said he worked late and went out of town on business more than any other member of his law firm. Allen categorically denied that he had ever been unfaithful to Darlene. He insisted that she was a very sick, suspicious woman. He accused friends and neighbors of being spiteful gossips who tattled to Darlene.

Darlene was no longer listening. She had made up her mind to leave after years of pretending to believe Allen. She didn't come to counseling to save their marriage; she came to work out the arrangements for their separation. I helped them design a structured separation. Allen begged her to reconsider. For the past ten years, she had pleaded with him to spend time with her. Allen had lost the opportunity to save his marriage. He no longer had the power to persuade Darlene. The time for negotiation, cooperation, and change had finally ended. Allen was shocked; he thought Darlene would always be waiting for him when he decided to return home. He was mistaken. Darlene had emotionally left the relationship.

I was the medical examiner for this couple. Darlene had emotionally left the relationship; it was dead. We explored the hopes and dreams that had brought them together. Although it is painful to look at the pathogens that destroy a relationship, we struggled through that also.

The failure of a relationship can never be attributed to one partner or one cause. Darlene's contribution was responding to Allen's extramarital pursuits by hearing, seeing, and speaking no evil. By refusing to face a painful truth, she colluded with Allen. Darlene had two regrets. One, that she had not drawn lines in the sand at the beginning of their marriage. Two, that she had waited ten long years to terminate a painful, humiliating charade. After our sessions, Allen retaliated by openly dating other women.

Here are the manipulative techniques Allen used in an attempt to avoid responsibility.

ALLEN'S MANIPULATIVE TECHNIQUES

Blaming: Manipulators know that body language counts. "His facial expression said, 'See what I have to endure from this woman.'" He was trying to blame Darlene and to gain my sympathy. "He accused friends and neighbors of being spiteful gossips who tattled to Darlene." Darlene was not the only person he blamed; he spread it around. Allen was trapped and he knew it. Blaming is frequently the last-resort manipulative distraction.

Begging: This is another last-resort strategy; however, some manipulators, especially hostile men, find it especially effective. Allen is appealing to Darlene's emotions; it has probably worked for him in the past.

Retaliation: "Allen retaliated by openly dating other women." This is normally an after-the-fact ploy used to embarrass and hurt the other party.

Starring the Womanizer

Why don't we begin with a Rhodes Scholar Player, former president Bill Clinton? Mr. Clinton's two terms in office were scarred by various charges of philandering. He certainly fits the profile of a Player; he is attractive, charming, and likeable. A generation before Mr. Clinton, another handsome president, John F. Kennedy, was said to have enjoyed the companionship of many lovely women. Interestingly, Vice President Johnson bragged that he got more women by accident than Kennedy did on purpose.

In the days before "tell-all about Monica's underwear" news reporting, it was whispered that Kennedy's conquests included the troubled, sultry star, Marilyn Monroe. Terry Teachout (2003) wrote, conceivably with a touch of sadness, "We discovered that the crown prince of Camelot was a reckless womanizer." Robert Bork writes in the *National Review*, "The American people elected Bill Clinton twice, knowing that he is a womanizer . . . many Americans appear not to care about morality in government." Possibly, Americans believed that Mr.

Clinton's sexual idiosyncrasies were private and did not affect his leadership ability.

Joseph Catania, a behavioral epidemiologist suggests that about 28 percent of men President Clinton's age (52 at the time) have had affairs. Presidents Kennedy and Clinton were charismatic, fun-loving, genial men . . . we didn't want to believe they were Players, because we honestly liked them. Say it ain't so, Joe.

In fiction, the quintessential ladies' men are handsome, adventurous, and courageous: Captain Rhett Butler of Charleston and fascinating, suave, debonair, and lover extraordinaire James Bond. In movie after movie, beginning in the 1960s, 007 managed to survive the onslaught of stunningly beautiful and excitingly treacherous villains. Unhappily for Rhett, he fell in love with the indomitable Scarlett O'Hara, a woman with a few Player tendencies of her own.

Dealing with the Womanizer or the Player

First, you must decide, after weighing the evidence, if your lover is a Womanizer. If you have sufficient evidence to prove that he is, then I would suggest learning more about his history. Normally, unless there is a life-changing experience (he comes perilously close to being shot by an irate husband), past behavior is the most accurate predictor of future behavior. If he has an established pattern of short-term mating strategies, I am not optimistic about change until he reaches late middle-age.

I know one Womanizer who has reached half a century and is still active and disturbingly successful. He isn't alone. Leigh, Temple, and Trocki (1993) reported results of adults surveyed in 1990 on the number of sexual partners respondents had had during the preceding five years. Approximately 6 percent of the study subjects had had multiple partners in that period.

In his extramarital sex (EMS) survey for men, Dr. Weiderman (1997) reported that the lifetime incidence of extramarital sex increased with age up to the oldest age group surveyed, at which point the incidence decreased. Therefore, age was a relevant indicator. Men who had accumulated the most affairs over time were somewhat older. Perhaps, members of the oldest group grew up before the sexual revolution of the 1960s. Multiple sexual relationships were not as socially accepted, certainly not publicly, during the early to middle years of the twentieth century. Womanizers exist and they are obsessed by their sexual pursuits. Multiple relationships serve a purpose, other than just the pleasure of sex. If you have any hope of discouraging your mate's behavior, he needs to understand the purpose that womanizing plays in his life. Then he needs to find another less-troublesome activity to satisfy that need. For example, if he is addicted to the adrenaline rush, he may want to try the following:

- Mountain climbing
- Car racing
- Stock brokering
- Piloting a plane

If he plays because he needs to bolster his ego, one of these activities may work:

- Going back to college
- Getting counseling
- Finding a cause that excites him (i.e., the environment, championing children or the elderly, politics)

It is possible that he will not want to change. If that is the situation, then you have two choices: (1) accept him as he is, or (2) move on to a more balanced relationship. More than likely, you will not have to make the decision; he will move on when the next challenge presents herself.

Keep in mind that he is an expert at creating the reality he wants you to believe. Unfortunately, that reality is less substantial then the reflection in your mirror. He is Merlin the Magician, hiding behind a concoction of prevarications and skewed truths. I know from clinical experience that you can possess an intense, heart-shattering passion for an illusion. When you convince yourself that you love his "altered reality" and not him, you have taken a vital step toward independence. Very possibly, the man you absolutely adore does not exist. I suggest buying the single "I Will Survive" by Gloria Gaynor. This song will help you replace the pain with indignation. If you search, you will find anger deep within you. Allow it to surface.

1. **Be fair, reasonable, and forgiving.** There is much variety in this type. Some Womanizers have a long list of phone numbers and misbehaviors. Others have strayed once; some accused womanizers are entirely innocent. Try to have as many facts as possible before you confront your wandering (?) man to avoid unnecessary conflict. According to our Constitution, he is innocent until proven guilty. You will have to decide when to be forgiving. Many variables will probably be involved in making this decision, such as: length of relationship, his qualities, if children are involved, your financial resources, and how motivated he is to make changes.

2. **There must be consequences for his behavior.** Our society does not excuse or encourage infidelity . . . usually. There are career, social, and personal consequences imposed on unfaithful spouses. How you respond is also a consequence. Behaviors that are followed by negative consequences are less likely to be repeated. The negative consequences should be unpleasant enough to have some bite, otherwise he may ignore them.

Some consequences must be imposed by the unfaithful man. Does he feel guilt? Is he angry with himself? Does he wish it had never happened? Did he think about how you would be affected if the relationship was discovered? Is he in emotional pain? Loving two people can be extremely painful. The lone affair by a person of character can be a devastating experience for everyone involved. Listen to each other.

3. **Don't be swayed by excuses.** If he is a serial Womanizer he is also an expert at creating and delivering excuses. Excuses have worked for him, so he will continue to use them. He will deny everything, admit nothing, and demand proof. You are not required to play that game. It is okay to request that he provide proof since his veracity is in question for a very good reason . . . he has been untruthful and deceitful. If he has admitted an affair and is sincerely attempting to rebuild your relationship and your trust in him, the situation is quite different from a Womanizer who denies, avoids, and lies. His excuses may be genuine reasons for being late or going out of town. Unredeemed Womanizers have a stock of excuses, such as . . .

- I had to work late.
- My car broke down (ran out of gas, had a flat).
- I was visiting a sick friend.
- We are just friends.
- It is not me, it is you. You are too suspicious.
- I was working out at the gym.

Sometimes, probably most of the time, these excuses are true. However, when they become the norm rather than the exception and you have evidence of truancy, unsupported excuses are no longer suitable.

4. **Be consistent.** A Womanizer is not consistent (except in womanizing) and you do not know what to expect from

him. However, he needs to know exactly what to expect from you. If you say, "I will not accept excuses without proof," then that should be your statement every time the situation arises. If you make exceptions, he will take advantage of them and you are back at square one. It is difficult to stand your ground when he is loving and caring. He knows how to manipulate your emotions. Don't allow it.

5. **Choose your battles carefully.** You don't enjoy confrontation, arguments, and hostility. You probably want peace and quiet (and you deserve it). So, make your life easier by choosing carefully. It is okay to ignore the small stuff. Your primary goal is to have a monogamous relationship with your guy. Choose battles around this issue. Dropping his clothes on the floor can probably wait until later.

6. **The Blame Game.** He will try to distract you at times by blaming you for nagging him. He might say, "If you weren't such a nag I wouldn't go looking for other women." Or, "I am innocent and you are paranoid." Don't fall into that common manipulative trap. You are not required to defend yourself. If you refuse to play, the game ends very quickly.

7. **Strength in numbers.** You need support. Yes, it is very hurtful to have to admit your man may be cheating on you. I would share this information with only a trusted few, very few. You can get support in other ways. Just spending time with people who love and value you will raise your self confidence and your mood. Be sure to do that whenever possible; look for opportunities. Call friends and suggest meeting for coffee, lunch, dinner, a movie, or just baking a few cookies and enjoying each other's company.

   Your Womanizer is probably not making you feel valued or beautiful. You are valuable and you are beautiful. Your friends and family will be delighted to show you how much you mean to them. Soak it in; you need it.

The Bottom Line

Many of us spend our whole lives running from feeling with the mistaken belief that you cannot bear the pain. But you have already borne the pain. What you have not done is feel all you are beyond the pain.
◄ *Saint Bartholomew*

How will you know when it is time to leave the relationship? If you have evidence that he is a player (and you are a trophy) and you have learned about his sexual history, then you also know his future—and yours. No one can tell you how you should respond. The choice is yours alone and it won't be easy.

If you decide to seek a relationship with a trustworthy man who deserves you, tell your friends. They can be there for you as you wander confused and saddened through your dark emotions.

Also, friends, family, and coworkers can encourage you to become an active participant in your social group again. This is not a time to be alone. Please don't sit and listen to love songs that remind you of your ill-starred love. Eating comfort food will not fill the void. You deserve better than that. Tighten your belt, pull up your boots, and keep moving. The road ahead is bumpy.

Now, let's see if your man is a Womanizer or a Player.

The Womanizer or Player Test

Are you ready for the test? Remember, some of these behaviors can be interpreted in various ways; some interpretations are entirely innocuous. However, if your man has multiple indicators, you may want to discuss the test results with a rational and logical family member or friend.

1. Does he frequently work late?
   Yes ○   No ○

2. Have you been told that he is having an affair?
   Yes ○   No ○

3. Is his appearance especially important to him?
   Yes ○   No ○

4. Have you found evidence, such as lipstick on his clothing?
   Yes ○   No ○

5. Is he frequently gone without explanation?
   Yes ○   No ○

6. Do your friends hint that he is unfaithful?
   Yes ○   No ○

7. Was he unfaithful in previous relationships?
   Yes ○   No ○

8. At the beginning was he "too good to be true"?
   Yes ○   No ○

9. Does he minimize your concerns about other women?
   Yes ○   No ○

10. Does he say that you are overreacting?
    Yes ○   No ○

11. Have you caught him in lies?
    Yes ○   No ○

12. Has he stopped treating you as if you were special? (Which, by the way, you are.)
    Yes ○   No ○

13. Does he become angry if you question his excuses?
    Yes ○   No ○

14. Does he use intimidation (i.e., threats, yelling, physical coercion) to manipulate you?

Yes ○   No ○

15. Do you make excuses for his behavior?

Yes ○   No ○

16. Do you "want" to believe his explanations even when they are not logical?

Yes ○   No ○

17. Does he flirt with other women when you go out together?

Yes ○   No ○

18. Is he egocentric?

Yes ○   No ○

19. Is he evasive and secretive (i.e., e-mail, cell phone, about where he has been)?

Yes ○   No ○

20. Would you describe him as competitive?

Yes ○   No ○

21. Is he insensitive to your needs?

Yes ○   No ○

Note also that questions 15 and 16 are behaviors frequently found in women who are in manipulative relationships. If you answered yes to both or either of these, please reconsider your behavior. It enables him to be dishonest. You may still the waters for a while, and I honestly understand why you want a semblance of normalcy. However, experience with couples has taught me that the day will come when payment is due.

Scoring the Test

Give one point for each yes answer; on questions 2, 4, and 7, however, count two points for each yes answer. Add up the points.

Scores 1 to 8

These scores indicate a slight chance that he may be having multiple relationships. Again, the scores may mean something completely different. A low score may also mean that you are in the early stages of your relationship. Some indicators develop later as a Player's interest wanes. Discuss your yes answers with someone you trust; do some reality-testing. Most of the behaviors mentioned on the test are not conducive to a thriving, healthy monogamous relationship. You might want to consider your yes answers as a therapeutic to-do list. It is okay to talk to him about what you need and to expect consideration and cooperation. If he is not inclined to be obliging, I suggest that you consult a marriage counselor.

Scores 9 to 15

These scores indicate it is certainly possible that your partner is unfaithful. However, you are the one interpreting each question. Therefore, before you do anything else—again, please reality-test. Then, if you decide that you have sufficient reason to be suspicious, you probably do. If you confront him, it is highly improbable that he will simply confess and ask for forgiveness. It could happen, and that would be a positive indicator that he may change, but don't be disappointed if it does not happen. After calmly discussing your concerns, be prepared with a plan B.

At this point, an objective third party could be of invaluable assistance in helping you and your partner untangle the web of deceit in your relationship. This is not going to be brief therapy; it will require a commitment from both of you.

Congratulations, you have taken the first step.

Scores 16 to 25

We have not proven guilt. He may still be innocent. However, the likelihood of innocence is growing smaller. Again, as with the former groups, please reality-check your answers with someone you trust to be candid and objective. It appears you have decided that you can answer yes to at least several of the questions. If they are correct, your partner has various behaviors and/or beliefs that make it exceptionally difficult to establish or maintain a loving monogamous relationship.

You will have to decide if you wish to work on the relationship or make changes as an individual. Even if you have concluded that your partner won't change (and he may not), counseling can be extremely beneficial. If you move outside your comfort zone, you will need empathic support to help you thrive in the emotionally turbulent days ahead. Remember, not making a choice is also a choice.

Myths about Affairs

Myth: All men have affairs.

According to Frank Pittman (1989), approximately 50 percent of men have affairs. And only about 20 percent are true Womanizers with multiple affairs under their notched belts. People routinely lie to investigators about infidelity, cautions Peggy Vaughan, author of *The Monogamy Myth*. "You cannot trust anybody on a subject like this." She believes that about 60 percent of men have had an affair at some time. Studies vary; however, they are clear on one point: Not all men stray. Don't accept it as an excuse.

Myth: An affair dooms a relationship.

Not necessarily. I have seen many relationships survive an affair. It takes commitment and a foundation of love; however, it can certainly be successfully done. Although, long-suffering wives frequently divorce men who desperately scamper from woman to woman. I have found that an affair often follows the death of a loved one, such as a parent. Perhaps the loss leaves an emotional void that he recklessly tries to fill.

Myth: The "other woman" is a sweet, young thing.

Sometimes this is true; quite often, it is not. The "other woman" comes in many ages, body styles, and degrees of beauty.

Myth: Most affairs are with coworkers.

"There is very little sex with coworkers." Joseph Catania (1998), a behavioral epidemiologist said that his study indicates that most affairs are with friends (57 percent) of at least six months, not colleagues (9 percent).

Conclusion

Womanizers and Players are resistant to change. They are also resistant to telling the truth. He may spin a beautiful story, but it is still a fairy tale. You would be happier reading a Grimm's

Brothers book; at least you know their stories are pure fantasy. There is one advantage to having a Womanizer in your life; he will tell you exactly what you want to hear. The disadvantage is that you might believe it.

Womanizers and Players are unquestionably attractive, interesting, and sexually experienced. They are not faithful, loyal, or responsible. Although many relationships survive quite well after an affair, multiple relationships are a death knell. If your man has had a single competing relationship, there is hope. In fact, I have seen marriages grow stronger than before, if the partners are able to talk about the affair and listen to each other's feelings. Anger is a natural reaction to pain. After a while, anger destroys any hope of a successful reconciliation. Some women find it impossible to get beyond the anger, and dissolution of the relationship becomes the only viable alternative.

Womanizers are annoying because of their testosterone overload and their obsession with the chase. The next group of manipulators is annoying because they have made a conscious decision to drive you crazy. Whereas Players are problematic for women, Passive-Aggressive men do not discriminate. At least, you are not the only target for their negative attitude, paranoid beliefs, and peculiar behaviors. Dependent Men and Mama's Boys may employ passive-aggressive behavior as part of their arsenal of manipulative tools. However, the next type has elevated it to an art form. In the next chapter, we will explore the psychological quirks of the quietly angry Passive-Aggressives and discover why they slowly and gleefully drive their partners to distraction. Let's meet the Passive-Aggressive.

CHAPTER 8

The Passive-Aggressive
Man

I like long walks, especially when they are taken by people who annoy me.
⊷ *Fred Allen*

I CALLED THESE MEN the Quietly Angry because they may not raise their voices, or actively confront, but they will drive you crazy. One reason that their behavior is so annoying to others is that you can't put your finger on what they are doing unless you notice their pattern of behavior. You can't say, "Don't raise your voice when we are talking," because he may not speak loudly. You can't say "Don't throw dishes when we argue," because he probably won't throw anything—at least not when you are watching. He is an expert at being annoying, making your life miserable, and generating countless headaches with few if any visible signs of anger. Their behavior may best be described as "plausible deniability." You will understand that when you attempt to prove they are purposefully annoying.

You might be thinking, "This isn't so bad, no screaming, no throwing things, sounds good to me." Make no mistake, he intends to make you feel wretched, one small incident at a time. His primary coping strategies are passive resistance, surface submissiveness, evasion, and circumventing of rules (Pretzer and Beck, Clarkin, and Lenzenweger, eds. 1996).

We aren't certain why individuals develop this exasperating behavior. However, it has been suggested that they were not allowed to express anger and to disagree as children; therefore, they learned to veil their aggression. They appear to believe that others are trying to control them, and they doggedly resist that control. If he makes you feel miserable, he is using passive-aggressive behavior to express his anger.

Do the following behaviors seem familiar to you? Does your partner have a few of these traits? Perhaps it is time to decide if he might be a passive-aggressive person.

Criteria for the Passive-Aggressive Man

To be diagnosed as passive-aggressive, he will need to have four or more of the following:

- Passively resists doing routine social and work-related tasks
- Complains that others do not understand or appreciate him/her
- Acts sullenly and argues with others
- Criticizes and scorns authority figures (parents, spouse, teachers, bosses, etc.) without reason
- Expresses envy and resentment toward persons who are better off
- Exaggerates and complains a lot
- Exhibits a consistently negative attitude

- Fails to do his or her share of the work or does substandard work on purpose
- Procrastinates
- "Forgets" to do something on purpose

(Source of first four behaviors, the Medical College of Georgia's Web site, *www.MCG.edu*)

Since the Quietly Angry folks tend to be negative and uncooperative, relationships with them can be fraught with tension.

Individuals with Passive-Aggressive Personality Disorder (PAPD) struggle between their desire to act out defiantly and their awareness that they must curtail their resentment. They engage in grumbling, moody complaints, and sour pessimism; these behaviors serve as both a vehicle for tension discharge (relieving them of mounting anger) and as a means of intimidating others and inducing guilt (Ekleberry, 2000).

There are effective ways to reach the Quietly Angry and to help him see his maladaptive behavior as the interpersonal stumbling stone that it invariably is. We will talk about those strategies later.

Case Study #1: David and Susan

David and Susan have been married for twelve years and have two daughters. They were schoolmates who married right after graduation. Susan soon realized that David would disagree with anything she said. He would make promises he never kept and sulk if she tried to talk to him about his broken promises and unfinished projects. Susan wanted to keep her marriage together for her children, so she coped with David's behavior and hoped he would become more cooperative as he matured. This dialogue was repeated many times each week, only the subject changed.

David and Susan discuss getting their house ready to sell while sipping coffee in their kitchen.

> SUSAN: According to the real-estate salesman, Jeffrey, if we paint the inside of the house it will sell more quickly. I think he has a good idea.
>
> DAVID: Well, of course, you think it is a good idea. It wasn't my idea. What does Jeffrey know? Does he have a crystal ball or something? I think the paint looks just fine.
>
> SUSAN (thinking-here we go again): David, we really need to sell the house before school starts. We should do anything that will help it sell.
>
> DAVID: We don't have the money to paint. I work all the time, but we never have money. You should remember that you had to have a new car. We might have a little money if you had waited. I knew we would need that extra money each month. Remember, I told you not to buy a car?
>
> SUSAN: David, could we just stay focused on the problem at hand?

David sulks to the den and plants himself in his recliner where he stays the rest of the evening.

DAVID'S MANIPULATIVE TECHNIQUES

Whining: "Well, of course, you think it was a good idea. It wasn't my idea." The general message is that Susan is unfair and that he has been, and continues to be, wronged. He sends the same message in various ways.

Blaming: "You should remember that you had to have a new car. We might have a little money if you had waited." "I work all the time, but we never have money." He is saying in various ways, "This is your fault."

I am the only one who is competent: "I knew we would need that extra money each month. Remember, I told you not to buy a car?" This is another way to blame Susan and at the same time elevate his position.

Sulking: Whenever David decides he is not winning the current conversation, he sulks and refuses to talk, except in grunts, until Susan gives in. This can be a very effective strategy.

Let's look at other traits indicative of the passive-aggressive disorder or of a wannabe.

Don't think that his quiet rage is channeled only toward you. No, Passive-Aggressive Men drive their coworkers and employers crazy too. Dr. Mark Unterberg describes how passive-aggressive individuals derail efforts to increase their efficiency: "A key characteristic is the increasing frustration of coworkers and supervisors who try to encourage more productive activity. Meanwhile, the passive-aggressive employee seems to move calmly on, apparently unaffected by the surrounding inefficiency and irritation." (*www.managedhealthcare executive.com*) Interestingly, individuals with atypical depression (as opposed to other depressive disorders) are more likely to be passive-aggressive and obsessive-compulsive (*Clinical Psychiatry News* 26(12): 25). Therefore, you may want to watch for signs of depression. The *DSM-IV* describes atypical depression as "the patient with atypical features experiences mood reactivity, with improved mood when something good happens."

Early Names and Descriptions for Passive-Aggressive Behavior

In early literature, individuals similar to those covered by the designation of passive-aggressive personality disorder were referred to as:

- Dissatisfied people who acted as if they were perpetually wounded (Aschaffenburg, 1922)
- Fussy people with sour dispositions (Hellpach, 1920)
- Depressives with ill tempers who were spiteful, malicious, and pessimistic (Schneider, 1923)
- People with irritable moods (Bleuler, 1924)
- People who took everything hard and felt the unpleasantness in every situation (Kraepelin, 1913) (Millon & Radovanov, Livesley, ed., 1995, 314–316) (Ekleberry)

Case Study #2: Dennis and Sage

Sage and Dennis were slightly late for their appointment. Sage began to apologize as soon as they were in my office; she said Dennis is frequently late. They chose to sit on the sofa together.

Dennis is a sturdy man of forty-five who has owned a service station for fifteen years. Sage, thirty-five, helps him at work by ordering supplies, keeping the accounts balanced, and paying the bills. She is a slender brunette. They have been married ten years and have one child. Dennis was married twice before; both relationships ended in divorce. This is Sage's first marriage.

Dennis slumps down into the sofa and frowns at the world. Sage says she can't tolerate his negativity. She laments that he complains about everyone and everything including her, and never gets to work on time.

Dennis rolls his eyes and continues to slump. I notice that he looks tired and about twenty pounds overweight. I ask him what he would like to be different in his marriage. He says, "I just want to be left alone. I work all the time. What does this woman want?" He looks at Sage and sits up for a moment, but then resumes his sagging posture.

Sage says, "He sulks when he is upset with me, or with our son or with someone from work. He promises to do things and never does. When he does something, it is because I have consistently reminded him to do it. His lack of responsibility drives me crazy!"

Dennis looks at Sage. "You are evidently determined to make me out to be the problem. I don't have anything else to say."

Sage is close to tears. "This is what always happens. We never discuss or resolve anything. I am so tired of this."

Dennis's Manipulative Techniques

Individuals such as Dennis resist perceived attempts to control them. It is a reflex reaction; they feel pushed to do something and they do just the opposite, do "it" badly, or procrastinate. If Dennis understood how to be assertive, rather than passive-aggressive, he would be more successful in his relationships and in his career.

You might also notice that Sage has taken responsibility for Dennis' behavior. Repeatedly reminding Dennis to do something simply activates his oppositional response and he becomes entrenched in resisting Sage. It would save a tremendous amount of blood, sweat, and tears if Sage allowed Dennis to learn from the consequences of his behavior.

Cognitive-Behavioral Treatment for
Passive-Aggressive Behavior

I am aware that passive-aggressive individuals are more likely to have atypical depression, and I notice that Dennis is tired and overweight. Consequently, I suggest that he make an appointment with his physician for an evaluation. I make the suggestion, explain why I am making it, and the potential benefits. Then I leave the decision to him. If he is resistant, I can make the suggestion again later, when we have worked through some of the passive-aggressive behaviors.

If an individual has a contributing condition, such as depression or anxiety, couple's therapy is more complicated. I could not be certain how much of Dennis' maladaptive behavior was due to depression. As a bonus, if depression or anxiety is successfully treated, there will usually be a corresponding improvement in the relationship.

Cognitive-Behavioral Therapy (CBT) is frequently used in treating personality disorders, maladaptive personality traits, and couples. "Cognitive-behavior therapy (cognitive therapy or CBT) is used commonly in psychiatric practice to help individuals change the way they think (called 'cognitive restructuring') and behave in certain situations. Cognitive-behavior therapy is a widely accepted therapy that can be used to treat any uncomfortable or destructive habit or practice. It is commonly used to treat addictions, eating disorders, mood swings, stress, relationship difficulties, insomnia, anger, and other conditions" (Stoppler, *www.Medicinenet.com*).

If I used CBT in couple's counseling, I might ask the following questions to help clients understand how their thoughts affect their emotions and behaviors and therefore their relationships.

Cognitive Questions

Have you thought about our session last week? What do you remember most clearly? How does the relationship problem you are dealing with affect the following aspects of your life?

1. Your thoughts
2. Your behaviors
3. Your relationships with other people
4. How you feel

Individuals who are passive-aggressive normally do not understand the consequences of their behavior. Cognitive-Behavioral Therapy helps them to understand what they are doing, why they feel compelled to do it, and the hidden price tag attached to their behavior.

Starring the Passive-Aggressive Man

Major Frank Burns is the star of passive-aggressive television characters. In the long-running series *MASH*, Frank was the man everyone loved to hate. Even his lover, Hot Lips, came to realize that Frank simply wasn't worth the trouble. He was an inept doctor, a straying husband, and an unreliable lover. More than his fatigues were green. He was seething with envy, he was blatantly incompetent, and his co-surgeons Hawkeye and BJ were, to Frank's chagrin, knowledgeable, skilled, and compassionate caregivers. Since Frank could not compete with them in the operating room, he tattled on his "buddies" to the Army brass, pulled rank, and spied on them whenever the opportunity presented itself. I think we were all relieved when the ever-whining Ferret Face Frank packed up his soiled uniforms and flew home to the long-suffering Mrs. Burns.

Steve Martin had a wonderful passive-aggressive solution in one of his comedy roles. He said make a million dollars and when the IRS asked why you hadn't paid any taxes, "just say you forgot." Steve's lame excuse might be acceptable for most significant others and employers, however, I would not attempt it with the IRS.

Peter Falk played the sometimes passive-aggressive police lieutenant in the 1970s television series, *Columbo*. He used passive, even bumbling, tactics to move closer to his suspects. He aggressively gathered evidence even as the suspect smugly underestimated his trench coat–wearing rival. Somehow, Columbo always knew who committed the crime and spent the episode toying with him or her as a bored cat might amuse himself with a mouse. Columbo did not have a passive-aggressive personality. He simply chose to use those behaviors to reach a goal.

Dealing with the Passive-Aggressive Man

If your Quietly Angry person decides that his behavior is threatening his marriage, he may choose to do something about it. He may decide to take one of the following approaches.

He may take an assertiveness-training course. These courses are offered through many hospitals, colleges, high schools, churches, and community education programs. If he learns to be assertive, he won't need his passive-aggressive traits anymore.

He may try to gain objectivity. One way to do this is to reality-test with someone he trusts. Objectivity will make understanding the part he plays in his problem easier to recognize.

He may decide to tackle one problem at a time. For example, if he procrastinates at work, he can learn how to use his time more wisely. He can read self-help books or learn from someone who is very organized.

He may seek professional counseling if self-help does not work for him. He (or both of you) may need the help of a skilled therapist to learn to relate in a different, more relationship-friendly manner.

If your mate is unable or disinclined to attempt change, then you will have to decide on your course of action.

As you remember, the Quietly Angry are not particularly insightful and do not appreciate suggestions. If you urge him to try to help himself, he will probably resist. It might be better to tell him what you need from him. Be assertive, and then wait and see.

If, after a reasonable period, he has not moved toward insight and change, you can design your plan of action.

The Quietly Angry fear being dependent; therefore, they create distance. If you can interpret their maneuvering as a way to maintain their autonomy, not as a rejection of you, you may be less distressed when it happens.

1. **Be fair, reasonable, and forgiving.** Each time he gives excuses, lies, procrastinates, disagrees just to be obstinate, or forgets a responsibility or a promise, tell him how his action affects your relationship. You might say, "Dennis, you have promised several times to take my car to a garage. You have not done it. I feel sad and angry because my needs and concerns don't appear to be important to you."

   With this conversation, you have been specific about what he did, how you felt, and what you believe.

   The good news is that passive-aggressive individuals can and do change. It probably won't happen overnight. Nonetheless, he will find the power to change if he values the relationship. His history, the tenacity of his passive-aggressive tendencies, his resources, and the presence (or lack) of co-morbid disorders and other personality traits will also affect his capability for growth.

2. **There must be consequences for his behavior.** Maladaptive behaviors have negative consequences. They injure personal and business relationships. If you try to protect him from consequences, he will never learn from his actions. Allow him to learn and gain insight.

3. **Don't be swayed by excuses.** Passive-Aggressive Men are experts at creating excuses. In fact, a Passive-Aggressive first said, "My dog ate my homework." Words do not replace behaviors. Wait until he keeps his promise, and then give him lots of praise.

4. **Be consistent.** He is consistent. He consistently procrastinates, makes excuses, sabotages projects, and whines. You know what to expect from him. He should also be certain what to expect from you. Never say, "If you do that one more time, I am going to pack my bags and leave!" unless you have every intention of keeping your word. It is preferable to make a more benign promise, such as, "If you continue to be negative, I am going to go shopping at the mall." Remember, if you have written clear, concise rules and have given him a copy, then your response will not come as a catastrophic surprise.

   That does not mean he will applaud your organizational and communication skills. If you change the rules of the game (yes, it has been a game with unwritten rules), he will not be delighted. Since you do not have control over his emotions, don't accept responsibility for them. He chooses his responses and emotions; regrettably, he doesn't understand that yet.

5. **Choose your battles carefully.** Bob is a forty-two-year-old accountant. His wife, Sandra, is a high school history teacher. They have been married for ten tumultuous years. During a session, Bob announced that he had an idea that would reduce the discord in their marriage. He had decided

to argue with his wife on Thursdays. On the other days of the week, he would avoid arguments, by walking away if necessary. By doing this, he could cut his marital disagreements by six-sevenths. Sadly, there were a few problems with Bob's numbers-driven solution. One, his wife would not agree (she was not an accountant). Two, their disagreements would never be resolved. Three, if he could adhere to a peaceful solution six days a week, why not seven? Four, Bob's blood pressure would rise during the ceasefire.

Bob simply wanted peace; so, one issue was no more worthy of combat than another. Most of us, especially those of us who are perfectionists, will make a stand and dig in our heels over small issues. Let me suggest that you write a hierarchal list of concerns and resolve them one at a time.

If you begin to feel stressed by the tortoise-like pace of change, throw on your best sundress, some cute sandals, and head to the nearest coffee shop. After a scone (or two) and some cappuccino, you will find your balance again. It will be even more fun if you ask a friend to go with you.

6. **Avoid the blame game.** Externalizing blame is a major indicator of passive-aggressive tendencies. Therefore, you can depend on its happening. The solution is easy; do not accept blame unless you are in fact responsible. Let's go back to Sage and Dennis. If Sage bought a car, she should accept responsibility (Yes, I bought a new car. Now, may we return to the issue?). Notice that she *did not* accept responsibility for financial difficulties. Dennis can learn how to respond adaptively when Sage models appropriate, mature behavior.

Attempting to place the blame on Sage (obviously he doesn't want to paint anyway) is a diversionary tactic. It is the emotional equivalent of setting off a smoke bomb. Sage doesn't need to defend herself. She has tried that in the past (so have you). Did it help? *Hint:* People make mistakes. We are human. Perfection is boring and annoying. Knowing whom to blame is not a solution. Refuse to play that game.

I never blame myself when I'm not hitting. I just blame the bat and if it keeps up, I change bats. After all, if I know it isn't my fault that I'm not hitting, how can I get mad at myself?
~ *Yogi Berra*

7. **There is strength in numbers.** Remember that friend with whom you sipped cappuccino at the coffee shop? Having these individuals in your life to share laughs, pains, and the minutiae of life is spiritually healing.

   Much blaming and criticizing goes on in a home that harbors a Quietly Angry person. These caustic traits poison the air you breathe just as surely as chlorine or sarin gas. You need a consoling, accepting environment to clear your lungs and to remind you that most relationships are not toxic.

8. **Evaluate your strengths and weaknesses.** We all have our strengths and our weaknesses. Relationship skills can be feeble or robust, depending on our interpretation of their value. Notice that independence is on the same continuum with intimacy.

Independence_____healthy_____intimacy_____

Since you are reading this chapter, I must assume your partner has not yet arrived at a healthy balance. Nonetheless, he has exhibited some aptitude for intimacy or you would not have fallen in love with him. Humans yearn for closeness, even when they steadfastly cling to indifference.

We have strengths because we have cultivated them. They were important to us at some time in our lives. In your mate's early life, independence may have had survival benefits. Now, that early protective skill is maintaining a painful loneliness in your relationship. Any effort to brave his fear of intimacy will move him closer to the middle. With patience, persistence, motivation (his)—and, perhaps, an experienced therapist—your relationship can grow. I promise.

The Bottom Line

You have modeled appropriate behavior, resisted pushing or criticizing him, made him aware of self-help options, and assertively asked for what you need, and nothing has worked. You cannot find a distinguishable iota of growth. There is scant evidence that he yearns for propinquity.

You cannot take full responsibility for your relationship, even though you may believe you can "save" it if you just try a little harder. At some point, and only you know where that point lies, hope dwindles. Ask yourself some questions and pay very close attention to your answers:

- What is the very least that I will accept in a relationship?
- How much am I willing to invest?
- What is my ideal relationship (that is still reasonably attainable)?
- How close am I to that relationship?
- What are my options?
- Do I love him?
- What do I love about him?
- Can I grow in this relationship (reach my potential)?
- Can I be myself?

After you have considered these questions, then consider the realties of life. *Realities* may include financial survival, children, where you will live, whether you have an adequate support system, and many other essentials.

Talk with friends, consider options, and give yourself time to adequately evaluate your situation. I wish you happiness.

There are men who are also vain, egocentric, and occasionally ruthless. They make wonderfully successful businesspeople and politicians. Learn more about them in the next chapter.

The Passive-Aggressive Test

1. Does he frequently procrastinate?
   Yes ○   No ○

2. Is he negative and woebegone much of the time?
   Yes ○   No ○

3. Does he blame others for the misery in his life?
   Yes ○   No ○

4. Does he seem to do things wrong on purpose?
   Yes ○   No ○

5. Has he had issues due to his negative attitude at work?
   Yes ○   No ○

6. Is he less successful than he might be due to his inability to work with others?
   Yes ○   No ○

7. Does he blame his employers and coworkers for his career problems?
   Yes ○   No ○

8. Does he have few, if any friends?
   Yes ○   No ○

9. Is he resentful and critical of authority?
   Yes ◯   No ◯

10. Does he resist doing anything you ask of him?
    Yes ◯   No ◯

11. Does he frequently sulk?
    Yes ◯   No ◯

12. Has he been diagnosed with depression?
    Yes ◯   No ◯

13. Does he frequently use the excuse "I forgot" to avoid taking responsibility for his actions?
    Yes ◯   No ◯

14. Does he spend more time complaining than doing his share of the household chores?
    Yes ◯   No ◯

15. Have you thought that his behavior is adolescent?
    Yes ◯   No ◯

Scoring the Test

Give one point for each yes answer.

Scores 1 to 5

The scores in this group are low, and that means either he has few of the passive-aggressive tendencies or you have been very kind in scoring the test. A man can be relatively moody or sulky and have this many (or more) passive-aggressive traits. Unless he also has traits from other maladjusted personality types, he should be amendable to change if he is committed to your relationship. "Gentle" is the best strategy at this low score level. Tell him how you feel about him and your relationship and why you want him to adjust his behavior. He may have some requests to make also and this gives him an opening. Perhaps you simply want moderation in some behaviors. List the behaviors you consider maladaptive and tell him what behaviors you prefer. If he frequently "forgets" chores or promises, ask him what the two of you can do to remedy that issue. It is possible he is simply getting forgetful; sadly, that is not unusual in our hurried and aging population. Remember to compliment him on his loving behaviors.

Scores 6 to 10

He has a moderate level of passive-aggressive tendencies, but he is still amendable to change. Follow the suggestions for the former scoring group. If that doesn't lead to positive changes, talk with him again about the behaviors you are targeting and add the natural and/or imposed consequences. If he still "forgets" his household responsibilities, stop helping him and, perhaps, consider not doing some of your chores. A consequence should have teeth, so he must feel some inconvenience if one of your chores is left undone; otherwise, it won't be an effective consequence. If this does not work, consider couple's counseling.

Scores 11 to 15

It appears that your mate has many if not all of the traits associated with the passive-aggressive personality. This is not necessarily a death knell for your relationship. Again, humans are very adaptive and positive change can happen.

Naturally, you would immediately like to begin working toward a romantic, loving, and supportive relationship. Begin slowly and work your way up to a cooperative alliance, if that is possible. According to marriage therapist John Gottman, there are four Grim Reapers of behavior that indicate a relationship is leaping headfirst into the abyss (or words to that effect). The first is *criticism*; avoid it at all cost. You can make a complaint and certainly should, when it is indicated. A criticism attacks your mate; a complaint tells him how you feel and how you are affected by his behavior. The next Grim Reaper is *contempt*. Contempt says to your mate, "You are worthless." Address the behavior rather than attacking the individual. The third is *defensiveness*. It says, "I didn't do it. Even if I did do it, you have done worse." Defensiveness will accept no responsibility; it simply points back toward you. The last Grim Reaper is *withdrawal*; this is the adult equivalent of putting your fingers in your ears and humming when your mate is trying to talk to you.

Certainly, you don't want to do these things. If your mate employs one of these behaviors, immediately stop the interaction. This is a good time to say, "Maybe we should talk later." Stay calm and relaxed by taking deep breaths or relaxing your muscles. Remind yourself that you are in control when you choose to walk away. Schedule another time to talk.

Conclusion

What are the advantages of having a Passive-Aggressive Man in your life? Let's see, he is negative, spiteful, and envious; he procrastinates, sulks, and disagrees with everything you say. I would suggest asking him to talk to his physician. If he is depressed, which is entirely possible, medication and therapy could make a positive difference in his behavior. After you are assured either he is depressed (and will seek treatment) or he is not depressed, you are in a better position to judge his merits. If he is willing to listen to your concerns without defending himself, you will have a very positive indicator. If your Passive-Aggressive sulks when confronted and will not discuss issues, you have an almost-insurmountable roadblock.

The Narcissist is in some ways similar to the Passive-Aggressive Man. The Narcissist sulks, he is attached to his role and resistant to change, and he is frequently envious and negative. He simply ties it in a much prettier package. Let's meet the Narcissist.

CHAPTER 9

The
Narcissist

Pride is a powerful narcotic, but it doesn't do much for the autoimmune system.
ᴏ Stuart Stevens

NARCISSISTS LIVE TO BE admired and flattered. If you are willing to feed their insatiable appetite for attention, approval, and affirmation, you will probably get along quite well. Whereas most of us enjoy positive attention on occasion and will work toward that goal, Narcissists constantly scan the environment looking for their "supply." They lack normal insight; their presentation is grandiose and inflated. Admitted Narcissist and authority on that personality type, Dr. Sam Vaknin says, "If these—the adulation, admiration, attention, fear, respect, applause, affirmation—are not forthcoming, the narcissist demands them, or extorts them." The Narcissist will desperately seek positive attention. Or, if that is not forthcoming, he will accept negative attention, achieved in whatever manner necessary. Perhaps it was a Narcissist who said, "Any publicity is good publicity, as long as they spell your name right."

If you are in a relationship with him, you will be of little importance in his life other than providing his supply of attention. Since you are of minimal importance, meeting your needs will not be a high priority. The more narcissistic traits he has, the more he will fit this description. If he has very few of these personality traits, he may sincerely esteem your relationship. The narcissistic personality may be arranged in an infinite number of configurations. Some are more lovable and flexible than others.

Narcissistic Personality Disorder (NPD) was named after the Greek mythical figure, Narcissus. He was the son of the river Cephissus and the nymph Liriope. According to Julia Kristeva's *Tales of Love*, "As he tried to quench his thirst . . . he saw an image in the pool, and fell in love with that unbodied hope, and found a substance in what was only shadow." If I understand this correctly, he fell in love with his reflection. Exclusive preoccupation with self is the defining feature of Narcissistic Personality Disorder. Is it really love?

The essential feature of Narcissistic Personality Disorder is a "pervasive pattern of grandiosity, need for admiration, and lack of empathy that begins in early adulthood" (*DSM-IV* 1996, 658). These are unique individuals. They comprise only 1 percent of the general population. Therefore, your mate may have some or many of the characteristics of NPD and not qualify for the disorder. An individual's degree of narcissism can vary from virtually insignificant to severe.

Narcissists are a study in contrasts; they believe that they are entitled to special treatment and that they should be successful. In fact, some do succeed in their profession, because they pursue success with single-minded determination. They are also heavily invested in their physical appearances and may become maudlin and desperate as they age; this is not a situation you want to experience.

Many of the personality types mentioned in this book are incredibly proficient at shooting themselves in the foot (and anyone standing close to them). Unfortunately, they don't learn from their errors; thus, they are destined to repeat the same sabotaging behaviors indefinitely. Their irrational beliefs and emotional immaturity haunt them throughout their lives. Though the Narcissist has limitations due to his self-serving, egocentric, grandiose belief system, he is capable of achieving success. In fact, he can succeed on a grand scale. If you were to look at a list of the 100 most successful men in America, a hefty percentage of them probably have narcissistic tendencies. No doubt, a few would meet the criteria for Narcissistic Personality Disorder.

Narcissists can be brilliant at accruing capital and building empires and yet have tense, disconnected personal relationships. Because Narcissists lack empathy, they can only conceive of intimacy as an abstract concept. Intimacy requires the ability to listen intently, comprehend what the other person is saying at an intellectual and emotional level, and effectively express your perception. Narcissists live within the confines of their egocentric world; other humans function as props for the Narcissist's performance. In their worldview, props are meant to be functional (I would like a cup of coffee, and don't you think I am fascinating?). Props do not require empathy or intimacy.

Not all narcissistic individuals or wannabes are successful. Although they have the desire for success and sincerely believe they merit success, they lack the innate ability to achieve it.

Criteria for the Narcissistic Personality

- Grandiose sense of self-importance
- Preoccupation with fantasies of beauty, brilliance, ideal love, power, or limitless success

- Belief that personal uniqueness renders them fit only for association with (or understanding by) people or institutions of rarefied status
- Need for excessive admiration
- Sense of entitlement
- Exploitation of others to achieve goals
- Lack of empathy (does not recognize or identify with the feelings and needs of others)
- Frequent envy of others or belief that others envy them
- Arrogance or haughtiness in attitude or behavior
- Reluctance to accept blame or criticism
- Absence of altruism, though gestures may be made for appearance (Kantor 1992, 203–204)
- Shallowness (Francis 1995, 374)

(Based on Morrison, *DSM-IV Made Easy*, 1994)

Masterson (1981) said that NPD individuals have a state of emptiness, rage, and envy. They are reactive and withdraw at the slightest perceived slight. They can experience such inappropriate rage in response to someone diminishing their sense of superiority that they attack and attempt to destroy the source of criticism (Oldham 1990, 93–95). Some Narcissists who do not meet the full criteria can function well and be almost free of symptoms. However, this type of Narcissist will still have unusually high expectations for himself. Since it is impossible to meet his expectations consistently, he will be dissatisfied with his life.

Identifying a Narcissist is not difficult once you become aware of the personality traits. Does this description sound like your mate?

Case Study #1: Darren and Rachel

A telephone conversation between Darren and Rachel:

> RACHEL: Darren, can you pick up the children from school at three today. I have to deliver a presentation. The person who was supposed to deliver it is home sick. The after-school snacks are in the refrigerator. I should be home by five o'clock.
>
> DARREN: You must be kidding! You know how much I have looked forward to playing golf with George today. He is such a poor player. He wants to learn my strategy for playing an awesome game.
>
> RACHEL: Yes, I understand your disappointment. I would not ask if it were not an emergency.
>
> DARREN: If I remember right, you are the one who wanted children. I told you they take up a lot of time and are very expensive. If it weren't for my extraordinary gift for marketing real estate, we could not pay for their private school and all the lessons they take. You will have to find a way to pick up them up; call one of your friends. This is not my problem. I am late now. *Click.* He hangs up.
>
> RACHEL: Darren, Darren . . .

Darren manipulates Rachel without really thinking about it. As far as he is concerned, his plans are important; Rachel's career and the children are not.

DARREN'S MANIPULATIVE TECHNIQUES

Me-centered arrogance: "You will have to find a way to pick them up." Darren is too important to bother with minor details. "You must be kidding"; in other words, I can't believe that you are bothering me with this.

Pompous disregard: Darren will do what is important to him, so naturally he will play golf. Rachel is left to wonder why she married him. Rachel's concerns and the children do not exist; after all, he is late.

Blaming: "If I remember right, you are the one who wanted children," and "this is not my problem." Consequently, this little situation must be Rachel's fault.

Grandiose self-importance: Darren is, according to him, entitled to special consideration. He reminded Rachel of his unique gifts: "my extraordinary gift for marketing real estate; my strategy for playing an awesome game."

The Antisocial or Psychopath might take pleasure in distressing Rachel, or winning the battle. Darren does not. Her feelings are immaterial to him. In fact, he is probably not aware that she has feelings or that his egocentric indulgence may come back to haunt him. Can you anticipate Rachel's mood when Darren returns home from his golf game?

The Successful Narcissist

Narcissists succeed because they have an overpowering drive to impress others. They will move heaven and earth, if necessary, to be loved, admired, and affirmed.

A successful Narcissist can put on a pleasant social face to attract new admirers; this is called the *false self*. Maintaining the fiction of the false self requires acting ability that would be the envy of most Academy Award–winning actors. Narcissists learn to mimic genuine emotions, such as compassion, caring, and love.

Another useful tool in preserving the false self is *illusion*, the ability to alter the truth while maintaining a shallow facade of reliability and authenticity. They may even believe some of their falsehoods. Narcissists are frequently pathological liars.

Once an admirer is drained dry and can (or will) no longer provide the admiration the Narcissist desires, she is cast aside. It must be a staggering shock to see the real Narcissist once the mask is removed. The experience must be akin to Dorothy peeking behind the Wizard's elaborate false self and stumbling head-on into reality. The great Wizard was simply an ordinary human being.

The Unstable Narcissist

The Narcissist embraces his false self. He must continually scheme and recreate himself to keep reality at bay. His fragile ego cannot accept less than perfection. Therefore, he reacts with rage to any suggestion, no matter how trivial, that he may be flawed. His extreme reaction comes as an unpleasant revelation for the unsuspecting bystander.

Since you can't fool all of the people all of the time (according to Abraham Lincoln), the Narcissist lives in fear of discovery. Emotional instability is the price he pays for constant deceit and vigilance.

Case Study #2: Jake and Ally

I was pleased to see Jake and Ally when they arrived (late) for their first session. Jake was a striking man, tall, well dressed, and attractive. I noticed that Ally had been biting her fingernails and her dress was buttoned wrong. She was obviously focused on something other than her appearance. Her hair looked as if she had just awakened from a troubled night's sleep. Under other circumstances, she would have been considered a very pretty woman. I knew from their intakes that Ally was a thirty-year-old high school teacher. Jake, also thirty, was a successful stockbroker.

I looked at Jake again; not a single hair was out of place. I was amazed that he could project such a flawless appearance.

Jake spoke first. He apologized for being late. It was Ally's fault. He hates to be late, but she cannot seem to get herself together. He said, "You would think since she takes forever dressing that she would look more polished." Ally glared at him, and then looked back down at her hands. Jake continued, "Can you believe that she used to be beautiful and exciting? Just look at her now! When I chose her, she was the perfect companion and business hostess for me. All of my associates congratulated me on finding such a jewel. Do you think I introduce her to a business associate now? Not likely . . . ."

I was watching to see how they interacted.

Ally finally spoke, "I don't know what to say or what to do. Nothing is ever good enough for Jake. No matter what I do, Jake gets angry and yells."

Perhaps to support the truth of her words, Jake yelled, "That is because you can't think. You silly cow, if you would use a little logic—after all you have a degree—then you would not make stupid mistakes and embarrass me."

I decided that it was time for me to speak. "Jake," I said, "I appreciate your trusting me enough to show me how you react to Ally at home. Do you think that your behavior will enhance your relationship with her? Can you think of behaviors that might work better?"

Jake just stared at me. He grabbed his car keys off the table and stalked out of the office, slamming the door. I believe that was one of my shortest sessions. Ally began to cry and said, "Do you see what I mean? He blows up for no reason."

Yes, I saw.

JAKE'S MANIPULATIVE TECHNIQUES

Jake wanted to control Ally's behavior. He'd bought a Barbie doll, and then discovered that she had a mind of her own. She was important to his self-image. Ally was an extension of Jake, much like his expensive suits and trendy sports car. According to Jake's belief system, if Ally was not perfect, then neither was he.

Intimidation: Jake harped, yelled, and scolded to "make" Ally become perfect again. At one time, he'd probably used *compliments* and *charm* to keep her in line.

Blaming: Jake insisted that their problems were Ally's fault.

Avoidance and denial are the defense mechanisms that Jake employs to maintain his false self. When he realized that I was not going to support his intimidation, he probably decided that I was not special enough to recognize his uniqueness.

If we had had more time, we might have been able to establish a workable therapeutic relationship. There are certain aspects of Jake's life that merit admiration.

Starring the Narcissist

We could probably choose any male Hollywood star in the past fifty years for our famous Narcissist. Oh, there are two exceptions: Tom Hanks and Jimmy Stewart. Sam Vaknin, author of *Malignant Self Love,* said that Erich Fromm diagnosed both Hitler and Stalin with Narcissistic Personality Disorder. I find it difficult to entirely agree with Erich Fromm. I believe psychopath would be the primary diagnosis. Yes, a person can meet the criteria for both disorders. Psychopathy, much to the chagrin of psychopath super-sleuth, Dr. Robert Hare, is now cast in with Antisocial Personality Disorder in the *Diagnostic and Statistical Manual of the American Psychiatric Association* (*DSM-IV-TR*). This is an ongoing difference of opinion. If you would like to know more, read Dr. Hare's intriguing book, *Without a Conscience,* and decide for yourself.

> *Narcissist:* psychoanalytic term for the person who loves himself more than his analyst; considered to be the manifestation of a dire mental disease whose successful treatment depends on the patient learning to love the analyst more and himself less.—THOMAS S. SZASZ

> The narcissist does not victimize, plunder, terrorize and abuse others in a cold, calculating manner. He does so offhandedly, as a manifestation of his genuine character.—VARDIN

When one thinks Narcissist, Donald Trump springs to mind. He is a hugely successful executive and now, a television personality. His ex-wife, Ivana, calls him *The Donald.* Ben Dattner, organizational psychologist and president of Dattner Consulting, said that "Narcissists can make tough decisions without being distracted by empathy, sadness or guilt." Does this describe Trump's secret of success? Ask Ivana.

The Narcissist cares only about appearances and attention. "What matters to him is the facade of wealth and its attendant social status and narcissistic supply. Witness the travestied extravagance of Tyco's Denis Kozlowski. Media attention only exacerbates the narcissist's addiction and makes it incumbent on him to go to ever-wilder extremes to secure uninterrupted supply from this source {attention}" (Vaknin UPI, 2002).

Does this dialogue sound familiar? "Why do they still write me fan letters every day? Why do they beg me for photographs? Why? Because they want to see me! Me! Norma Desmond!" Have you seen the old movie *Sunset Boulevard* (1950)? Norma Desmond is an aging actress who lost her audience when talkies (movies with sound) replaced silent movies. She maintains a false self (the belief that she is still famous and adored). Unfortunately, Joe Gillis, a writer, unknowingly challenges her false self. In Norma's mind, a romance develops between her and the youthful Gillis. Later he is found at the bottom of her swimming pool. One does not stand between a Narcissist and his/her false self.

Notice in the following dialogue that Joe Gillis, exploiting his perilous ignorance of narcissistic volatility, steps where angels fear to tread:

> **JOE GILLIS:** You're Norma Desmond. You used to be in silent pictures. You used to be big.
>
> **NORMA DESMOND:** I *am* big. It's the *pictures* that got small.

Yes, Norma, spoken like a true Narcissist.

Of course, Hollywood is the perfect incubator for narcissism. Hollywood was wrought from the essence of its greatest natural resources: fantasy, egotism, and a philosophy of life straight from *The Emperor's New Clothes*. Could megastars such as the late Marlon Brando and Madonna fit into the Narcissist mold? "Wary of the gap between the false and true self, the star overcompensates by developing a God complex" (New York Metro, 12264).

Are Narcissists naturally attracted to the Gold Coast Land of Oz or do they convert after the initiation rite? The answer is probably a complex combination of factors, but that is another book.

Dealing with the Narcissist

Depending on your mate's quantity and quality of narcissistic traits, it may be relatively easy to enlist his cooperation or it may be virtually impossible. Let's begin with relatively easy. There are two things to remember about individuals with egocentric tendencies: (1) Anything he does must have a payoff in love, adoration, or attention. (2) Try not to disturb him with references to the real world; remember, he is doing all he can manage to sustain his false self.

A successful Narcissist once confided to me that he spent all of his waking hours helping the needy. In reality, he did spend many hours each day visiting the sick and picking up groceries for the elderly. However, he didn't do it because he was altruistic. He did it as part of his "I am a saint" performance. He was exceptionally believable. I would have voted for sainthood. As usually happens, his false self could not be maintained, and his less saintly behaviors became public knowledge. Keeping the mask firmly in place had required a huge investment of energy.

Your boundaries should be very clear. In other words, your Narcissist or Narcissist wannabe must understand which behaviors are not acceptable. Be very clear about this; talk to him about behaviors (listening to what I say) not concepts (being more attentive). He is unlikely to spend time pondering why you are displeased. Make it effortless for him; write a contract specifying the targeted behaviors you discussed with him. Otherwise, he will probably say, "I don't have time for this." Your contract might look something like the following.

1. **Be fair, reasonable, and forgiving.** Nothing else will work, because he will not change unless he decides it is in his best interest. Applaud each change he chooses to make, no matter how insignificant. He will like the attention, and you may get even more cooperation. Keep in mind, Narcissists are like cats; they cannot be trained or coerced.

2. **There must be consequences for his behavior.** Perhaps you'll get the most success from applying positive consequences for all behavior that can be construed, even tenuously, as teamwork.

Targeted Behaviors
- "I love it when you really listen to me (turn off the TV, put away the book, look at me)."
- "I feel so warm when you hug and kiss me before you leave for work each day. You are a great hugger."
- "I feel wonderful when you tell me you love me. You are such a romantic."
- "I love to show you off when we go out on a 'date.' I would enjoy doing that more often."
- "Spending 'quiet' time with you is wonderful. I can never get enough of you."
- "I like to show you off at parties. So, when we go to a party, I think I will hang around with you more."

This format is effective because it focuses on one concept (being more attentive) and specifies which behaviors are included in "being more attentive," and it shows your mate in a favorable light. I have intentionally left some targeted behaviors open. When possible, show him what you want. For example, when you attend a party with him, stick like Velcro. After you have enjoyed enough time together, move on to other people. Remember to praise him. The easier you can make cooperation, the more likely you are to get it.

Below you will find a chart representing Maslow's Hierarchy of Needs for the average human being. However, note where it changes for Narcissists. Usually one must begin at the base of the hierarchy. For example, one must have physical comforts before one is interested in security. For the Narcissist, the most compelling layer is social acceptance. Though he is not striving for mutual love, togetherness, and teamwork, he desperately seeks recognition by family, friends, and total strangers. His esteem comes from reflection. He is not capable of personal esteem; he exists only in the acceptance and admiration of others.

Self-actualization, the final stage a person reaches in maturity, is only a vague concept for the Narcissist. He will not rise above social acceptance. Therefore, the positive consequences you apply should come from this level.

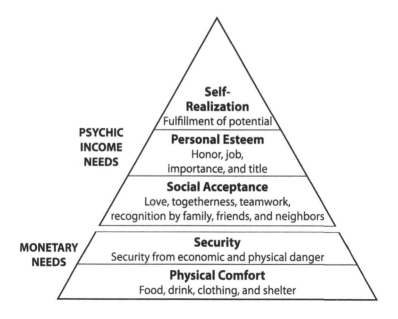

3. **Don't be swayed by excuses.** Wait until he does something to reward him. Promising to do something, if he finds the time, is not a change. Thank him for making the promise, and then wait until you see results.

Saying, "I would have done it except . . ." does not relieve your mate of responsibility. The following statement is from a probable Narcissist who is trying to avoid the unpleasant consequences of his behavior: As you can see, spying was not his fault (it was *somebody else's*).

If you want to do these people a favor who have problems—and I'm talking from experience—say something. If somebody had said something to me and put a block in front of me and said, "I think Jeff's got a problem and I don't think that he's handling it very well," that would have been enough to stop the process. . . . I lost everything—my dignity, my freedom, my self-respect.—Jeff Carney, Convicted Spy

Unless caught behaving in a manner that is inconsistent with their false self, Narcissists will probably not offer excuses. They are more likely simply to refuse to do "it" because they don't want to, and you should have known better than to ask. Narcissists are incapable of loving, and they fear abandonment. In fact, at times, they will leave a relationship to avoid potential rejection.

4. **Be consistent.** Continually ask for what you want and consistently praise his positive behaviors. I know that consistency requires time and effort. So, as a cop once told me, pull up your bootstraps, tighten your belt, and persist.

5. **Choose your battles carefully.** This guideline is especially true with Narcissists because any changes you request may be perceived as criticism. They do not respond well to criticism, real or imagined. You will not win cooperation using a frontal assault.

6. **Avoid the blame game.** Naturally, he will blame you. He cannot be at fault; so you must be. Ignore the blame, do not defend yourself, and keep putting one foot in front of the other.

7. **There is strength in numbers.** One simple way to determine if your mate has a personality disorder is to be aware of how you respond to that person. If you find that you are constantly confused and wondering if you are going crazy, then he has a personality disorder.

Narcissists live in a fantasy world, and they are very persuasive. By definition, they must be able to persuade others to adopt their skewed perception of reality. The longer you live with a person who has a unique, anomalous vision of himself, the world, and you, the more reasonable his outlook will appear to be. Discussing your beliefs and concerns with an objective third person can help you avoid this consequence.

Therefore, you need friends to help you stay centered as you attempt to improve your relationship. Otherwise, you will begin to wonder if you are the problem.

The Bottom Line

Again, you are not responsible for his behavior; you cannot change him. You can ask for change, encourage change, and work on changing yourself, but that is the limit of your power. I have known individuals who spent a lifetime earnestly attempting to alter or rescue someone. Husbands, wives, and parents frequently believe they can save their loved one from an addiction. This might be a good point to mention that Narcissists often have a dual diagnosis (narcissism and an addiction to a substance).

If your mate has a substance-abuse problem, insist that he seek treatment. If he does not, you may be in danger of arrest or harm if he continues to break the law. This is a perilous issue. I suggest that you have a discussion with an addictions counselor as soon as possible. Be armed with knowledge.

The Narcissist Test

Is your mate a Narcissist? Take the test and find out.

1. Does he react to criticism with feelings of rage, shame, or humiliation (even if not expressed)?
    Yes ○   No ○

2. Is he interpersonally exploitative (i.e., takes advantage of others to achieve her/his goals)?
    Yes ○   No ○

3. Does he have a grandiose sense of self-importance (i.e., exaggerates achievements and talents, expects to be treated as "special" without appropriate achievement)?
    Yes ○   No ○

4. Does he believe that his/her problems are unique and can be understood only by other special people?
    Yes ○   No ○

5. Is he preoccupied with fantasies of unlimited success, power, brilliance, beauty, or ideal love?
    Yes ○   No ○

6. Does he have a sense of entitlement (i.e., an unreasonable expectation of favorable treatment)?
    Yes ○   No ○

7. Does he require attention and admiration to bolster his self-esteem?
   YES ○   No ○

8. Does he lack empathy (i.e., an inability to recognize and experience how others feel)?
   YES ○   No ○

9. Is he preoccupied with feelings of envy?
   YES ○   No ○

Scoring the Test

Give one point for each yes answer.

Scores 0 to 4

Sorry, not enough points to meet the criteria for Narcissistic Personality Disorder. Maybe this person is genuinely extraordinary and unique; in which case, he or she does not have a disorder. In fact, I prefer to believe that everyone is special. Maybe that is why some unkind people (they probably have Paranoid Personality Disorder) call me Pollyanna. With our current information, we can say without fear of contradiction that this person is not boring. He may be a Narcissist wannabe who has some of the traits but not most of them. Since he has fewer traits, he may be willing to make some changes to improve your relationship.

Scores 5 to 9

Ah, we are certainly getting closer to a diagnosis. Again, we will not know without an assessment by a mental health professional. The degree of severity is important also. If I am

"He (narcissistic individual) is perceived to be asocial at best and, often, antisocial. This, perhaps, is the strongest presenting symptom. One feels ill at ease in the presence of a narcissist for no apparent reason. No matter how charming, intelligent, thought provoking, outgoing, easy going and social the narcissist is—he fails to secure the sympathy of his fellow humans, a sympathy he is never ready, willing, or able to grant them in the first place" (Sam Vaknin, *The Malignant Self-Love*). ❦

tenacious, it is a virtue. If I carry it to an extreme, it is stubbornness or inflexibility. Where is the line? Professionals have difficulty finding the line and sometimes miss it altogether. Frequently, psychology is more of an art than a science. The last statement of criteria says, "I show arrogant, haughty behaviors, or attitudes." Another way to phrase it would be "I show self-confidence, poise, and assurance." Again, where is the line?

(Source of the test and score analysis, *The Ultimate Book of Personality Tests*, McCoy, 2005)

Conclusion

"Even in Hell he (Narcissus) found a pool to gaze in, watching his image in the Stygian waters."
◡ᓚ *Ovid*

Beware; Narcissists are enamored with change and chaos if these conditions help them retain their position on center stage. Changing partners with chilling regularity is not unusual.

Pleas for change must consider his fragile ego and be framed in a positive way. *Reframing* is an effective tool to employ with a narcissist. Reframing simply means rewording an explanation or request in a way that is more acceptable to the person hearing it. Instead of saying, "You are self-indulgent and extravagant," you could reframe it. For example, "You have wonderful taste in clothes. It would be so disappointing if we maxed out our credit cards. Then you wouldn't be able to buy the new styles that are *so* you." Although you want to avoid throwing cold reality into the face of a Narcissist, he must face logical consequences at times. This is especially true if the consequences also affect you. If you decide to keep a Narcissist, you must be willing to make many accommodations to his personality. Remember, even if you are blessed with the intelligence of Einstein and the wisdom of Solomon, you may not succeed in improving or preserving your relationship.

Narcissists share many traits with Risk-Takers and Antisocials. In fact, there is no reason a man cannot be both (yes, a frightening thought). Both types are willing to reach their egocentric goals employing any manipulative technique available to them. Men who meet the diagnostic criteria for Antisocial or Narcissist are incapable of giving or appreciating love. Psychopaths as defined by Dr. Robert Hare are also incapable of understanding or experiencing love. Love is a means to an end because women in love are easy prey. Diagnosable Psychopaths come in three basic models: Bad, Worse, and Worst. Look under his hood and you will find a powerful 421-cubic-inch police interceptor engine. However, don't even consider using the brakes or kicking the tires. If the brakes ever worked, they stopped working long ago and the tire treads are treacherously thin. Nothing is more exhilarating than careening down a steep, curved mountain road at eighty miles an hour—with no brakes. If that imagery sends chills of excitement up your spine, you just might enjoy the Psychopath. If it causes you to break out in a cold sweat, skip the next chapter.

CHAPTER 10

The
Psychopath

Whoever fights monsters should see to it that in the process he does not become a monster. And when you look long into an abyss, the abyss also looks into you.
⟜ *Friedrich Nietzsche, 1886*

PSYCHOPATHS ARE EXTREMELY interesting men—from a distance. The diagnosis *psychopath* is no longer in the *Diagnostic Manual of the American Psychiatric Association* (*DSM-IV*). No, I don't believe psychopaths have disappeared from the face of the earth with the great dinosaurs. *DSM-IV* cast them into the Antisocial Personality Disorder diagnosis. However, according to Dr. Robert Hare, psychopath hunter extraordinaire, they are quite different from their cousin the sociopath (although they can be both).

Antisocial Personality Disorder refers to a cluster of criminal and antisocial beliefs and behaviors. Antisocial does not mean shy and retiring; it means in opposition to the rules of the society in which one lives. Antisocials often find themselves in prison, because they have difficulty adhering to the laws of the land. Psychopathy, according to Dr. Hare, "is defined by a cluster of both personality traits and socially deviant behaviors" (*Without Conscience* 25).

Do you know a Psychopath? It is disturbing to ponder; nonetheless, there is a very strong probability that you know one or more individuals with psychopathic tendencies. Approximately one out of every 100 people will qualify for Dr. Hare's criteria for psychopathy. I am not referring to serial killers who terrify you at the movies. They are exceptionally rare (thank God). You are more likely to be kidnapped by tree-hugging, tofu-eating terrorists than encounter a Dr. Hannibal Lecter.

One writer described Psychopaths as "soulless beings." This description conjures up images of long white fangs, a deathly pale complexion, and a black opera cape. Psychopaths look just like the rest of us; in fact, they are often considered quite attractive by the opposite sex. In 1941, Dr. Hervey Cleckely wrote the classic volume *The Mask of Sanity* describing psychopaths. Dr. Cleckely uses adjectives and terms such as likeable, charming, intelligent, great success with women; on their dark side, he says they are irresponsible and self-destructive. Please believe me, Dr. Cleckely is a master of understatement (McCoy, *The Ultimate Book of Personality Tests*, 2005).

Do you know someone who is too good to be true? Psychopaths are often fun, witty, charming, and charismatic. Some are extremely intelligent and highly educated. What makes them different from the usual manipulative man? They have no conscience and shallow emotional resources. Where will you find a psychopath? Everywhere. You are apt to find him in a boardroom, in a pool hall, in a classroom teaching college, in prison, behind the wheel of a patrol car, in an operating room, or in the pulpit on Sunday morning. Psychopaths adapt well considering their emotional limitations and self-serving life philosophy. They are in all socioeconomic and educational levels.

Criteria for the Psychopath

Since Psychopaths are everywhere, you may want to learn how to identify them. Here are a few warning signs from Dr. Robert Hare:

- Superficial charm
- Self-centered and self-important
- Need for stimulation and prone to boredom
- Deceptive behavior and lying
- Fraudulent and manipulative
- Little remorse or guilt
- Shallow emotional response
- Callous with a lack of empathy
- Lives off others or predatory attitude
- Poor self-control
- Promiscuous sexual behavior
- Early behavioral problems
- Lack of realistic long-term goals
- Impulsive lifestyle
- Irresponsible behavior
- Blaming others for their actions
- Short-term relationships
- Juvenile delinquency
- Breaking parole or probation
- Varied criminal activity

Psychopaths, Narcissists, and Antisocials (Exciting Risk-Takers)

If you have read Chapters 6 and 9 on Exciting Risk-Takers and Narcissists, respectively, you have probably noticed that Psychopaths have much in common with these two species of manipulative men. You may wonder how you can tell one from the others. Putting your mate in the right category is not important, because all three will suck the life out of relationships.

Nonetheless, as an academic exercise and because you might find it entertaining, I have compared these three scary manipulative types on the following chart.

Descriptive Criteria

Antisocial	Psychopath	Narcissist
Disregards others' rights	Shallow emotions	Grandiose
Aggression against people	Great actor	Unrealistic fantasies
Lying or theft	No conscience	Personal uniqueness
Serious rule violations	Arrogant	Needs admiration
Lacks remorse	Prone to boredom	Insecure
Runs swindles for gain	Predatory	Envies others

As you can see, these individuals have few problems exploiting others if it suits their agenda. In fact, exploiting is one of their favorite games. Of the three types, Antisocials are more likely to be arrested and sent to prison. Though Psychopaths are certainly capable of crime, even horrific crimes, they are less likely to be arrested. A successful Psychopath may even be brilliant and, perhaps, highly educated. This would be highly unusual for an Antisocial. They would find academia with its rules and deadlines inconvenient and annoying. A Narcissist loves himself and will ignore anyone who is not as unique as he is. However, he is probably the least likely of the three to bury the opposition in his backyard. In fact, I would be mildly surprised, but only mildly.

Antisocials are described by their behaviors, which are largely criminal, whereas Psychopaths and Narcissists are identified primarily by personality characteristics. This is not to say that all three types cannot exist in one individual. Antisocials who are also Psychopaths are definitely not rare creatures. The thought makes me shudder because this man would be a woman's worst nightmare.

Although Psychopaths are no longer in the *DSM-IV-TR*, they are distinct from the other types and deserve their own chapter. No matter where you find a Psychopath, you can be certain he will be leaving misery, bewilderment, and heartbreak in his wake. Dr. Robert Hare says, "They are . . . likely to be men and woman you know who move through life with supreme self-confidence—but without a conscience." Dr. Hare continues to paint the Psychopath's image, "He will choose you, disarm you with his words, and control you with his presence. He will delight you with his wit. He will smile and deceive you, and he will scare you with his eyes." If eyes are the windows to the soul, look into their eyes and you will see disquieting darkness where the soul should reside (McCoy, 2005). Let's examine some characteristics common to Psychopaths and Psychopath wannabes.

Glib and superficial: They can be intelligent, beguiling conversationalists (or speakers), and there is real passion in what they say. If you scratch the surface, however, you will find nothing beneath it.

Lack of empathy: Because their emotions are shallow, Psychopaths cannot understand emotions in others. If you hope to reach him by sharing your pain, forget it. He won't understand a word you are saying. You may notice that when he does express sympathy, sorrow, or grief (for someone else), his body language will not match his words.

Egocentric, narcissistic, and grandiose: He sees himself as the center of the universe. He has impressive ideas and plans, which are unlikely to reach fruition.

Deceitful and manipulative: With this man, what you see is never what you get. Psychopaths talk the talk. They do not walk the walk. He will instinctively understand your weaknesses and use them to reach his self-serving, idiosyncratic goals.

Lack of responsibility: His bills will probably not be paid on time, and he will not keep promises unless they are in his best interest or he is playing a part. He is not a Boy Scout.

Criminal or unethical behavior: He may very well have a rap sheet. You need to learn about his history. Knowledge is power. As always, when you attempt to analyze a psychopath, past behavior is the best predictor of future behavior.

Are Psychopaths Born or Raised?

Some brain studies suggest that Psychopaths have abnormal brain activities. They make certain connections more slowly than other children, show less fear of punishment, and seem to need to do things that excite their nervous system, such as thrill-seeking behaviors.

A few of the findings include:

- Adolescents who measured high on the Psychopathy Screening Device showed reduced electrodermal skin responses to distress cues in slides shown to them, indicative of a subnormal response.
- They also showed a decreased response to fear imagery and to threats.
- Personality traits related to psychopathy correlated with difficulty in processing emotional information.

- Psychopaths over-respond to distracters, showing reduced ability to focus and cognitive deficits in left-hemisphere activation.
- Psychopaths speak more quietly than non-psychopaths and tend not to differentiate between neutral and affective words; perhaps this means that they are insensitive to emotional connotations in language.
- Psychopathic adolescents respond more strongly to rewards than non-psychopaths; thus, they can sustain reward-producing activities for a longer time.

We aren't sure if Psychopaths are born or raised. However, it appears that both parenting and genetic issues play a part in creating a Psychopath. Of course, this is an academic discussion. If you live with a Psychopath, learning how he became what he is may not be high on your priority list.

Case Study #1: Alex and Lauren

Lauren, a friend and physician, quietly told me about her first meeting with Alex as we sipped our cafe lattes at Barnes and Noble. "A melancholy, rain-shrouded day foreshadowed our meeting. I sat in my comfortable overstuffed chair enjoying a few minutes of quiet reflection while waiting for my next appointment. Precisely at the appointed moment, I looked up to see Father Alex fill the door and then moved noiselessly into the room. His demeanor softly whispered "meek." Body language spoke of a man of faith humbled and stooped by the enormity of his task—bringing lost souls to salvation.

"I saw a man in his thirties who fell slightly shy of handsome. Probably, *striking* would be more a descriptive word. His sapphire eyes (jewels are beguiling, cold and hard) never wavered;

they stayed locked onto mine. A shiver scurried down my spine. Thick blond hair hung unfashionably to his shoulders. When he spoke, his voice was soft and reassuring. I was bewildered when the words *wolf in sheep's vestments* crept into my mind. At some intuitive level, I was aware that his cool appraisal and massive size were incongruent with his air of humble benevolence. *Incongruent* was a word I muttered to myself many times in the next few months. The truth is consistent.

After we talked for a few minutes about a charity-building project, he began to tell me about myself. He confidently assured me that I was beautiful, intelligent, witty, and successful. He said I frightened men. He also told me a heartrending story from his childhood. A primitive part of my mind watched, listened, and hissed, *Be alert! He is a womanizer . . . he has performed this little act before. He is an imposter pretending to be a human being . . . Beware, beware, beware . . .* I had an overwhelming desire to clap and shout, *Bravo! What a performance!*

Another part of me sternly admonished, *How can you be so judgmental? This is a man of God. Just look . . . see his meekness . . . his humility. Shame on you.*

For the first time since Lauren began the story, she looked up at me. I think I saw tears in her eyes, though I suppose it could have been a reflection. Her eyes were sad.

"I think you can guess which part of my psyche knew who and what Alex was. Hundreds of little red flags flapped briskly as if caught in a hurricane, bells screamed an all-out alarm, and I turned away."

Psychopaths, much like vampires, have vulnerabilities. They cannot successfully hide their true nature for extended periods. They simply must shoot themselves in the foot. Lauren and her community learned the hard way that Prince Charming can be egotistical, self-centered, dishonest, and pitiless. He was caught on camera with his hand in the proverbial till. Lauren was lucky;

she lost (temporarily misplaced) only her heart. Others lost their self-respect, their belief in basic human goodness, their spiritual guide, and financial resources. After a few months, Lauren recovered and went on to share a stable, loving relationship with a less exciting, but more deserving man. As we left the bookstore, Lauren confessed that a small part of her heart remains with the sweet wounded Alex who *never existed*.

How did Alex deceive an intelligent, intuitive, successful woman? Let's look at his tools of the trade.

Alex's Manipulative Techniques

Charming and complimentary: Alex told Lauren she was "beautiful, intelligent, witty, and successful." This was their first meeting; he did not know her from Adam's house cat.

False intimacy: By telling Lauren about herself, Alex made their "relationship" appear to be closer than it actually was. Remember, he was a stranger. Unfortunately, Lauren did not remember that.

Assuming an innocuous, safe role: Lauren used these adjectives to describe Alex: meek, humble, soft and reassuring voice, man of God, and stooped. It was not by accident that she saw these inoffensive characteristics. He intentionally projected them.

Exploiting emotions: Alex told her a sad story from his childhood. This also gave the impression that their "relationship" was more intimate than logic and reason could substantiate.

Manipulating the truth: Very little of what Alex said or projected was true.

Case Study #2: Edward and Emmy

Edward and Emmy sat as far away from each other as the physical limitations of my office would allow. I looked toward Emmy; she was petite, blonde, and furious. I wondered what had happened to trigger this response. Edward, on the other hand, appeared quite at ease, open, and friendly, although I did notice a slight "I must endure" smugness (a dead giveaway). Edward continued to smile his beautiful, white-toothed smile and Emmy glowered. I could feel the electricity crackling between them.

I asked a volunteer to tell me why they had decided to come to counseling. Emmy began reciting an extensive list of bizarre, egocentric behaviors and beliefs that she attributed to Edward. Emmy said she could not continue to accept the abuse Edward subjected her to each day. I was concerned because Emmy left no doubt that she was approaching her emotional limits.

Edward looked lovingly at Emmy and said, "Darling, I don't understand. I don't know how you can say those things about me. I would never hurt you. I love you with all of my heart." He then looked calmly at me and said, "We came to you because you have an excellent reputation and I knew you would be able to guide us. I am confident, just talking with you, that together we can help Emmy. She is overwrought. It has been extremely trying for her at work lately. You must understand that Emmy is very sensitive." Emmy's expression would have turned a lesser man to stone.

It was possible that Emmy was overly emotional, but it was equally possible that I was experiencing the manipulative behavior of a Psychopath. Emmy just looked at me, as if to say, "You believe him, don't you? He has done it again. I give up, I can't win."

Had it been my first encounter with a Psychopath, I might have been deceived. His manipulative techniques were not original or particularly brilliant; consequently, I was able to see through them.

As I learned more about their relationship, I supported Emmy in freeing herself before she became a casualty. I received an e-mail from Emmy a couple of months ago, and I was pleased to hear that she is healing. She enrolled in an excellent New England university and plans to get an advanced degree. Unfortunately, as I expected, Edward has snared another victim.

Emmy says Edward is dating a very successful television announcer who cannot or will not see through his charade—yet. Edward told Emmy he plans to marry his "friend." Then he struck suddenly, without warning, with hateful words, his supreme weapon: "I am so glad that I got away from you, Emmy. Now I have a sensual, sexy woman. Not a little mousy, drab drudge like you." Sorry, Edward, Emmy doesn't care what you say; she has been inoculated against Psychopaths.

Edward's Manipulative Behaviors

Cool composure: Emmy was distraught, yet Edward's emotional level was minimal; that is because he is a Psychopath. To an individual who is not cognizant of manipulative behaviors, Emmy would appear to have psychological and emotional issues and Edward would seem to be trying valiantly to reason with her. In fact, it is frightening to ponder how many times that ploy has worked in a therapy session. Edward made a point of focusing on Emmy's emotional reactivity. "She is overwrought. It has been extremely trying for her at work lately. You must understand that Emmy is very sensitive."

False intimacy: Edward attempted to pair professionally with me by saying, "I am confident, just talking with you, that together we can help Emmy"—even though we had just met and only one of us had a degree in counseling.

Manipulating the truth: Instead of answering Emmy's accusations, Edward simply denied them and focused on her perceived emotionalism.

Assuming an innocuous, safe role: Edward assumed the role of rescuer and pseudo-therapist.

Flattery: Edward attempted to pull me firmly into his corner by saying, "We came to you because you have an excellent reputation." Yes, it was manipulation. Why should he hesitate to manipulate the counselor?

Starring the Psychopath

There is little doubt that Scott Peterson, the convicted murderer who made us question our beliefs about the depths of depravity in human nature, is probably a Psychopath. If he did murder his wife and unborn son, he probably thought of it as a troublesome, yet necessary tactic to reach his goal of being with another woman. He may not have been angry. He may have just wanted his freedom and decided that murder was an appropriate tool to gain that freedom. Of course, what he gained was prison and notoriety.

This tragedy has spawned an interesting situation. Theoretically sane woman have written to Scott Peterson in prison hoping to inspire romantic ardor. "A prison spokesman said San Quentin received dozens of calls, letters and even two marriage proposals for Peterson" (Chris Erikson, *New York Post,* March 23, 2005).

This is not unusual behavior; many convicted murderers receive passionate messages from women admirers. The long list of romantically pursued killers includes John Wayne Gacy and Ted Bundy.

Although most famous Psychopaths (the ones who have been diagnosed) are murderers, they are the exceptions. The majority has not murdered anyone and may not have entered the criminal justice system at all.

Robert Hertz (2001) interviewed Dr. Robert Hare and made these comments:

> *Psychopathy may prove to be as important a construct in this century as IQ was in the last (and just as susceptible to abuse), because, thanks to Hare, we now understand that the great majority of psychopaths are not violent criminals and never will be. Hundreds of thousands of psychopaths live and work and prey among us . . . Your boss, your boyfriend, your mother could be what Hare calls a "subclinical" psychopath, someone who leaves a path of destruction and pain without a single pang of conscience.*

Dr. Hare's description of the Psychopath (remember he is the recognized authority on this personality disorder) and his numbers will make you take a closer look at your next new acquaintance. About one in 100 people will be a Psychopath.

Dealing with a Psychopath

Since Psychopaths are the most gifted of the manipulative types, you must counter their brilliant but illogical ploys with pure logic. He is a magnificent artist with words. However, as you pay more attention to what he is saying, you will note gaps in logic. These gaps are due to lies and smoke screen distractions. Cling desperately to facts (what he has done) and logical consequences. Lists are an effective way to look at these diverse bits of information.

So, let's be optimistic and focus on strategies and consequences.

1. **Be fair, reasonable, and forgiving.** First, simply talk about the violation and determine if you can come to a reasonable agreement. He must believe that it is in his best interest to agree. His question will be, "What is in it for me?"

2. **There must be consequences for his behavior.** What if he refuses to be reasonable? You know what is important to him. Use that information to choose consequences (it should make logical sense). For example, you want him to stop screaming at you. Also, you know he enjoys an audience. You could say, "If you raise your voice to me, I will immediately leave and return when you are calmer." This is an effective strategy because it applies a logical consequence to screaming at someone (the person leaves). Also, if an audience is important to him, then he doesn't want you to leave.

   Caution: No matter how well thought out and logical your strategy is, it still may not work. Individuals with psychopathic tendencies value "winning" at all cost. Manipulating other people to win is fundamentally who they are, as well as what they do. They play this game exceptionally well. Never bluff. If you aren't certain you will follow through, don't threaten.

   He will employ all of his techniques to avoid a perceived loss. Be prepared because the road may get very bumpy. Know when to walk away; a contest of wills could be dangerous.

3. **Don't be swayed by excuses.** When he says, "I didn't mean to raise my voice. I have had a terrible day. My boss just doesn't have a clue about selling. The idiot! Besides, I wasn't screaming." Yes, he was screaming. There are no acceptable excuses. The operative words were *I didn't mean to raise my voice.* He admitted it and then refuted it later in the same statement. This also is a psychopathic indicator. Sometimes their statements conflict. However, they do not seem to notice the irregularity.

4. **Be consistent.** As with all manipulators, stay your course. If you draw a line in the sand and then recapitulate, you will have accomplished nothing. If you say, "The next time you begin screaming I will leave until we can speak calmly," do it.

5. **Choose your battles carefully.** Decide what would make your life better, and stay with that issue. I recommend starting with something small to see how well he responds to a request for a change in his behavior. If he responds well, go to the next item on your list. If he does not, perhaps you need to rethink working toward change.

6. **Avoid the blame game.** Psychopaths and Psychopath wannabes are not responsible for negative outcomes or mistakes. He will blame you if it is convenient and mildly credible. He cannot accept blame unless it is part of the game. He might say, "Well, I would not have screamed at you if you had not made me so angry." Sorry, you cannot make him angry, happy, sad, guilty, or any other emotion. Do not accept blame for his behavior and/or emotions. You simply do not have that degree of power.

7. **There is strength in numbers.** To avoid feeling crazy when he blames you, has tantrums, gives excuses instead of promised behaviors, or any other manipulative techniques, turn to the people who are there for you. He may try to isolate you

from family and friends. Don't allow that to happen. You will need their support and their feedback for reality-testing.

Some people think only intellect counts: knowing how to solve problems, knowing how to get by, knowing how to identify an advantage and seize it. But the functions of intellect are insufficient without courage, love, friendship, compassion and empathy.
◐ *Dean Koontz*

The Bottom Line

Look at his behavior. If you did not see it or do not have pictures, it probably did not happen. Peering deep into his mind and attempting to understand his words beyond excuses and quasi-truths will just confuse and frustrate you. Have faith in verifiable evidence. This strategy will help you to feel in control and stable. He will hate that.

The Psychopath Test

Is your mate a Psychopath? It's important for you to know, so take the test.

1. Are there inconsistencies between his expressed emotions and body language?
   YES ○ No ○

2. Does he tell numerous lies, which he denies?
   YES ○ No ○

3. Is he bigger than life and charismatic?
   YES ○ No ○

4. Does he have a spotty employment history?
    Yes ◯   No ◯

5. Does he make remarks that are cold and callous and then say, "I was just kidding" (probably after seeing your reaction)?
    Yes ◯   No ◯

6. Does he act remorseless in circumstances that normally require an apology?
    Yes ◯   No ◯

7. Is he irresponsible about paying bills?
    Yes ◯   No ◯

8. Does he talk about impressive, unrealistic plans for the future?
    Yes ◯   No ◯

9. Does he enjoy risk and danger?
    Yes ◯   No ◯

10. Does he habitually blame others for his mistakes?
    Yes ◯   No ◯

11. Does he expect much more from relationships than he is willing to give in return?
    Yes ◯   No ◯

12. Is he secretive about his past?
    Yes ◯   No ◯

13. Does he refuse to answer e-mails or say very little in writing (having learned that e-mails can be used later against the person who wrote them)?
    Yes ◯   No ◯

14. Does he repeatedly cheat in relationships for the excitement and the challenge?
    Yᴇs ○   No ○

15. Is he secretive about his career and source of income (understandable if he is working for the CIA—which, by the way, does not exclude him from being a psychopath)?
    Yᴇs ○   No ○

16. Do others mention that he exhibits a dearth of discernable emotions (they may describe him as laidback, cool, unruffled—an android)?
    Yᴇs ○   No ○

17. Does he have a rap sheet (has he been arrested)?
    Yᴇs ○   No ○

18. Is he physically aggressive?
    Yᴇs ○   No ○

(Test taken from the author's *The Ultimate Book of Personality Tests*, 2005)

Scoring the Test

Give one point for each yes answer.

Scores 1 to 6

It is unlikely that he is a Psychopath, although it is not impossible. You may not have his complete history—yet. Considering the seriousness of the behaviors listed in the test, even a few make for an unhealthy relationship.

Scores 7 to 11

Unfortunately, the probability that your mate is a Psychopath is getting discouragingly high. Read your yes questions again. How do these behaviors affect your life? Let me suggest that you write the applicable behaviors on a sheet of paper and add the effect they have on your life across from the behavior.

After you have completed the list, you will more fully understand the investment you are making in this relationship. Is your compensation comparable?

Make a note of your yes answers. This is your list with all of the questions you answered in the affirmative.

Behavior (Yes answers)

- Habitually blames others for his mistakes
- Insists that everything wrong is my fault
- Refuses to listen to my side
- Alienates friends by insisting he is right even when he is not
- Loses jobs because he argues with his boss

The list of how his behaviors affect you might include (notice these are logical consequences of his actions):

How His Behavior Affects Me

- I have very few friends left.
- I am isolated.
- It makes me angry to be blamed for things he has done.
- I am tired of his anger when I try to explain my side.
- I feel intimidated.
- I feel as if I am walking on eggshells.
- I can't be myself anymore.
- I don't feel loved.

- I frequently change my behavior to avoid arguments that I can't win.
- He doesn't listen to me or value my thoughts or feelings.
- We have no financial stability.
- Our relationship is a game and he is winning.

Scores 12 to 17

I am sorry to tell you this, but it appears that you may have a Psychopath sharing your life. I suggest that you complete the behavior list from the previous scores. Considering the extreme nature of the behaviors mentioned in the test, there are serious problems in your relationship and in your life. Please talk with a good friend or therapist for some reality-testing. You deserve to be happy.

If you answered yes to number 18, you need to talk with someone at a safe house (women's shelter) as soon as possible. They will be able to provide the support and information you need to make your life safer.

Many experts agree that calling the police when a partner is abusive is a positive step. However, a 1992 study by R. Berk and colleagues indicated that arrest has a deterrent effect for a large set of "good risk" suspects, but there is a tendency toward increased violence in "bad risk" suspects. In another study that year, J. Hirschel's data indicated that arrest may still provide the appropriate response to these "incidents as non-arrest would convey the wrong message to offenders, victims, their children, and society in general. Sadly, there are no easy answers. The experts in many social areas are unsure about the value of mandatory arrest or what procedures *will* work for a woman seeking safety. This underscores the degree and prevalence of debate about domestic abuse.

I feel comfortable advising women to leave after the first incident. The abuse normally becomes more frequent and severe as time passes. As a psychotherapist, I have seen miracles happen in therapy sessions. However, I am not confident that spousal abuse group programs are particularly successful. Many studies have explored the diverse treatment programs. Although the studies vary on the percentage of repeat abusers, the recidivism rate after treatment is not encouraging. Some studies suggest that it may be as high as 100 percent.

Conclusion

Now you have a more comprehensive view of the parameters of your relationship. Change is possible; in fact, it is unavoidable. This is your opportunity to ponder which behavior changes would be most beneficial in improving your life.

When you talk with your mate about your needs and wants, he will characteristically ask what the payoff is for him before he undertakes accommodations. He is interested in stimulation, adoration, various addictions, and winning at all costs. You may want to word requests with this in mind. You may say, for example, "If you will do your share of the household chores (be very specific about which chores are his), I will help you clean your Mustang on Saturday." Or, "I noticed that a few bills have not been paid this month, I would be happy to take responsibility for our budget if you will stick to a limit on credit card spending."

Will he be likely to make concessions? Probably not, remember he is not housebroken; his talent lies in getting what he wants, when he wants it, and seeking pleasure. If you want to enjoy a fast-paced, stimulus-laden adolescent lifestyle, he is your man. If you want reciprocity from a responsible adult, you are bound to be disappointed. It will not happen.

However, if your mate has only a few weak psychopathic tendencies, you may want to design a strategy for improving your relationship. After you have clearly stated exactly what you want from him (and committed it to paper), consequences are next on the list. Behaviors have consequences, and those too should be made clear.

As with all other relationships, you have three options:

- Change the relationship (you need his cooperation)
- Accept the relationship
- Leave the relationship

There is a strong inverse relationship between egocentric, aggressive, or histrionic characteristics and the likelihood that they can be influenced.

We will next explore the psyche of the intimidating manipulator. He can come from any of the types; however, his most likely personality will be Psychopath, Antisocial, and/or Narcissist. Let's learn how to recognize, avoid, and eliminate the hostile manipulator.

CHAPTER 11

Understanding and Surviving
the Violent Manipulator

Reality? The reality is that no one is willing to draw a line in the sand. Nobody is willing to say that the law is the law. And if you break it, you will be prosecuted: win, lose or draw.
‑⌒ *Ben Stone,* Law and Order

ARROGANT MEN ARE AN ANNOYANCE. Narcissistic men and Womanizers turn our lives into a challenging game, as we attempt to stay ahead of their scheming, self-indulgent behavior. Beyond annoyance and challenge, we enter the darker side of human nature—violence. Hostile men would crush our spirits and redefine "who we are" as "who we should be." Their view of relationships is dominance driven and idiosyncratic. Manipulation is not confined to the clever and illusory. Intimidation is a crude, primitive form of manipulation employed by men who must control and dominate, much as other men must breathe.

In most cases, these men will not change and they certainly won't change to please us. Our goals must then be revised to accommodate this new circumstance (violence). Then, our new goals become (1) to avoid pain and injury and (2) to gain independence from the violent male. If you believe it is easy to leave a violent man, you have been given inaccurate information. Women in strongly aggressive relationships are more at risk when they attempt to leave or after they leave.

Intimidation is a ploy. Human beings are purposeful and intimidation has a purpose. It is used to get one's way without the inconvenience of considering fairness, intimacy, subtle persuasion (which is time consuming), good and evil, and the rights of others. A violent person (or one who threatens violence) probably adopted this manner of behaving because he witnessed it, was a victim of it, or perhaps he has faulty wiring. Intimidation is relatively quick, it frequently works, and it makes the intimidator feel powerful. Since intimidation does have rewards, the intimidator may be reluctant to try something gentler. Some personality types will choose to be violent when annoyed until they are too old to react physically. Be assured, attempts to avoid annoying them are destined to fail. Intimidators' rules are written in sand and they shift.

Information from the Texas Council on Family Violence defines abuse as "physical, sexual, emotional, economic or psychological actions or threats of actions that influence another person. This includes any behaviors that frighten, intimidate, terrorize, manipulate, hurt, humiliate, blame, injure or wound someone." As you can see, battering has many faces and numerous ways to cause pain.

Early Life: The Bully

It appears that violent men may have been bullying boys. The Center for Disease Control has targeted bullying as a health hazard. They broadly defined bullying as "a wide variety of behaviors, but all involve a person or a group repeatedly trying to harm someone who is weaker or more vulnerable." Their literature states that there are 5.7 million teenagers in this country and approximately 30 percent of them are involved in bullying as a perpetrator or a victim. This behavior becomes less prevalent as the young teenagers mature.

Stan Davis, author of *Stop Bullying Now*, agrees that bullying is not the exception; it is the rule at many schools.

Playground observation research finds:

- One incident of bullying every seven minutes
- Adult intervention in 4 percent of incidents
- Peer intervention in 11 percent of incidents

Physical bullying is defined as touching another student to create fear, to get one's way, or to feel powerful, or using physical strength in any act of aggression. Physical bullying includes hitting, kicking, biting, slapping, shoving, choking, and punching. Verbal bullying is also very painful for the victim. This type of bullying can include threatening, starting rumors, teasing, degrading and cruel jokes, extortion, stealing of money and possessions, and exclusion from the peer group.

Victims are adversely affected by bullying; they may become anxious and fearful and resist attending school. Victims may become more isolated, which can lead to depression. In extreme cases, the victim may become so depressed that he or she considers suicide an approximate solution. Feelings of self-worth can also be negatively affected. Residual issues may exist many years after the bullying stops.

This information from *A School-Based Anti-Violence Program*, a manual for families who have children in the criminal justice system tells us more about schoolyard intimidation (Suderman and Jaffee, 1996):

- Studies in several countries have consistently shown that at least 15 percent of students in schools are involved.
- About 9 percent are victims.
- About 7 percent bully others repeatedly.
- More students in younger grades are victimized.
- Boys are more likely to be bullies than girls.

This study data are easy to understand. The students most likely to be bullied are smaller or younger than the bully. Bullying isn't based on courage; it is based on cowardice. If we explore domestic violence, prison violence, or school violence, it is almost exclusively the strong exploiting the weak (due to size, age, gender, or number). The following data from recent research studies tell us which variables are commonly found in the bully versus bullied interaction: The following statements are frequently accurate, but there are always exceptions.

- Bullies are male.
- Bullies are physically stronger than their victims.
- Bullies are impulsive and confident.
- Bullies are aggressive.
- Bullies may come from homes where aggression is accepted.
- Victims are isolated.
- Victims are not assertive.
- Victims are shy and timid.
- Victims do not report to school officials (perhaps fearing retribution).
- Victims are less skilled and weaker than their bully.

Fortunately, bullying behavior is less prevalent as children get older. Bullying drops by about two-thirds from elementary to middle school. I was in elementary school and living in

Pensacola when I encountered my first bully. I can't remember the older girl's name, but I do remember she was enormous (or so it seemed to me).

Bullies should remember that children grow up. The child who was smaller than everyone else in elementary school may be a beefy weightlifter later in middle school. I once knew a bully named Tommy, who routinely tormented his younger cousin, Keith. The "little" cousin is now six-foot-four, 260 pounds, and a cop. Bullies burn bridges. They are impulsive. They don't consider long-term consequences. The same can be said of abusive men. They wonder, strangely enough, why they are emotionally disconnected. If an abuser is not alone, it is often because the woman in his life fears him. How very sad.

Picture this for a moment: Tommy is speeding along in his decrepit pickup truck (doing 60 in a 35–mile-per-hour zone), he sees blue lights flashing in his rear-view mirror and hears the ear-piercing wail of a siren. With unsteady hands, he pushes his beer under the seat, where it spills on the carpet. He straps on his seat belt and pulls over.

A mammoth cop slowly unfolds himself, one huge limb at a time, out of the squad car. All Tommy can see is yards of midnight blue uniform and dark shades. The officer lumbers toward the pickup and looks in. Tommy is already rehearsing his story. He jerks to his right when the cop taps on the passenger window. Tommy's smile turns sickly when the officer removes his shades and Tommy looks into those unsympathetic brown eyes. Yes, you guessed it—Officer Keith. The speeding Tommy story was just that—a story. It never happened. Nonetheless, it is fun to think about. The plight of bullies leaves many of us cold, as we emotionally recall the schoolyard bullies of our youth. Do you remember your first experience with aggression? Women who suffered from intimidation as children are more likely to accept aggression in adult relationships.

In working with adult women who were traumatized as children, I have discovered that creating a story such as the "Tommy Story" can be empowering. If you had bully (violence or intimidation) issues as a youngster, create a story that changes the power structure. As you remember the worst part of your true story, change it in a way that makes you strong and unbeatable (it doesn't matter how bizarre your change is). Use your imagination and creativity to write your story and read it often, until you no longer feel powerless when you remember that part of your early life experiences. Strangely enough, you will also notice a strengthening of your perceived power in the present.

Fortunately, schools are beginning to take these injurious experiences seriously and are earnestly attempting to rescue the bully and the victim. Many new anti-bully programs are being tested in schools around this country. Experiences such as the Columbine High School tragedy illustrate the reality of bullying. It is dangerous, and it must be adequately addressed.

Do Schoolyard Bullies Grow into Intimidating Adults?

Researchers hope to control violence by identifying the variables that influence the acceptance and implementation of violent behaviors. The list of possible variables is long and varied.

Dan Olweus, a Norwegian pioneer in the study of bullying research, found that eight-year-old bullies are five times more likely than other eight-year-olds to have a criminal record by the age of thirty (Paszkiewicz, *www.vision.org*). He does not say that the criminal record contains violent crimes; however, they are probably not white-collar crimes. Olweus's work also indicated that bullies were more likely than the average to have children who followed their parents' aggressive path.

A Danish study of five-to-seventeen-year olds (Sorensen and Jessen, 2000) concluded "children's fascination with violent computer games cannot be understood without considering these [social] aspects. The violent elements fascinate some children, but this fascination should not be mistaken for a fascination with violence in the real world. On the contrary, all children in the investigation repudiated real-life violence" (120). However, not everyone agrees. Recent court cases involving millions of dollars "have claimed that companies can be held liable if the content they publish plays a part in an individual's violent act, resulting in the loss of life" (Ontario's Office for Victims of Crime).

These changes in society's acceptance of violence may lead to a gentler, kinder future for us and for our children.

Other Contributing Factors

Many studies suggest that exposure to violent media images is a contributing factor in making a child more prone to be violent. Other contributing factors include a neurophysiologic predisposition, a violent environment, imperfect parenting, our history as a culture, and the proliferation of weapons in our society. All predisposing factors are pertinent and deserve attention.

Mental illness combined with substance abuse can be a dangerous mixture. Sue Davis, of the Arizona Alliance for the Mentally Ill, said, "The 1998 MacArthur Violence Risk Assessment Study {said} that people with both a serious mental illness and a co-occurring substance abuse disorder discharged from psychiatric hospitals were more prone to community violence than those with no substance abuse disorder." Substance abuse, without mental illness can also be a precipitating factor.

Why Men Batter

Jacobson and Gootman (1998) have studied violence to understand why some men batter. In the eight years of their study, their team made a number of myth-shattering discoveries:

- Batterers share a common profile: they are unpredictable, unable to be influenced by their wives, and impossible to prevent from battering once an argument has begun.
- Battered women are neither passive nor submissive.
- Batterers can be classified into two distinct types: men whose temper slowly simmers until it suddenly erupts into violence, and those who strike out immediately. This difference has important implications for women leaving abusive relationships.
- Emotional abuse plays a vital role in battering.
- Domestic violence can decrease on its own, but it almost never stops.
- Battered women do leave at high rates.

Millions of lives are touched by domestic violence each year. We can't afford to believe in myths. Studies such as this one illuminate the once secret world of domestic abuse.

Domestic Abuse and Alcohol

It is difficult to find one accepted reason that substance abuse has a strong positive relationship with domestic abuse. A correlation or relationship is not necessarily cause and effect. It just means as one increases, the other also increases. For example, during the hot summer months, more ice cream is consumed and more people drown. Obviously, neither causes the other, but they are both influenced by temperature. So, although we know that batterers are frequently substance abusers, we do not know that substance abuse causes battering (or vice versa). In fact, some studies suggest that even when a substance abuser stops abusing, he may still batter.

What if substance abuse and battering threads though the generations of a family? Does that mean that men can inherit a propensity for both types of abuse? Perhaps, but it may also mean that both are learned behaviors. According to a 1993 study by Kantor and Asdigian, parental substance abuse and parental *woman abuse* may impact the development of children, increasing the chances of a child growing up to be an abuser, a victim of abuse, and/or a substance abuser (Bennett, National Resource Center on Domestic Abuse). A gene linked to aggressive behavior may help explain why some men who were abused as children turn to violent crime while others do not. A new study suggests that men who have lesser activity of the gene called MAOA and who were mistreated as children are more likely to be aggressive than their peers who were also mistreated but have normal MAOA functioning (Marcus, *Health News*, 2004). Is there an inherited biological link to violent behavior? An earlier study found that people and mice that had no MAOA were prone to be aggressive. Scott Stoltenberg, a behavioral geneticist at the University of Michigan who has studied MAOA, said, "It's not genes or environment. It's definitely an interplay between the two, particularly in complex traits where many genes are involved."

Perception and Abuse

There are infinite realities. An abuser may interpret reality—specifically, their partner's behavior—as more "arbitrary, aggressive, abandoning, or overwhelming" (Bennett, 1997). It appears that this predilection for misinterpreting behavior is enhanced by substance abuse. In another report, Taylor (2004) said, "The effects of addiction may include distortion of information, misinterpretation of cues, persistent suspiciousness, irritability, impatience, paranoia, restlessness and delusion." If this is accurate, it certainly provides an interesting theory and suggests a treatment potential: to help batterers change the way they think. This theory, however, does not relieve batterers of responsibility for their actions, nor does it satisfactorily explain all hostile behavior. Many substance abusers are not violent; many violent men do not abuse substances. In a publication by the National Institute on Alcohol and Alcohol Abuse, a study compared non-violent and violent alcoholics: "Axis I diagnoses show alcoholic perpetrators have a higher proportion of anxiety related disorders than non-violent alcoholics." In other words, the pairing of an anxiety disorder, such as post-traumatic stress syndrome, and alcohol may trigger violent behavior. Other recent studies indicate that the correlation between addiction and battering is somewhere between 44 percent and 80 percent. Even the lower end of this range is a very strong positive correlation.

Learning about abusive men provides protection. It may help you identify a potential abuser before he becomes part of your life. The opportune time to walk away from a batterer is before he has the opportunity to abuse you. Our best decisions are based on sufficient, accurate information. I hope that right now, somewhere, a reader is drinking a great cup of cappuccino and saying to herself, "Hmmm, I think I will pass on this relationship."

Seeing the Warning Signs

I have asked women in abusive relationships if there were any warning signs or red flags early in the relationship. Most of these women said no. Yet, when we talk about the first few months of the courtship, we discover, to their surprise, that red flags were flapping.

Janet casually mentioned that her boyfriend, Sam, tried to throw her out of his car while traveling at sixty miles an hour. She explained away his responsibility for his reckless behavior by telling me that he was drinking. Sam promised Janet that he would never do it again. Promises are only as reliable as the person who makes them. Also, threatening to throw someone out of a moving vehicle is noteworthy evidence of an anger-management problem.

Janet is an attractive thirty-year-old insurance agent with two small boys from a previous marriage. Sam has the charm and dark, boyish good looks of the actor Tom Selleck. Unfortunately, charming or not, Sam does not play nicely with others. He is in his late thirties and hasn't settled into a career . . . yet. According to Sam, he has worked in numerous positions, but due to different external variables, he has not been successful. Near the end of the session, Janet thought for a moment and frowned. She mused, "It probably doesn't mean anything, but Sam can't seem to pay his bills on time. He owes back child support and a few car payments."

Janet and I discussed Sam's behavior and what it might mean to her as his girlfriend. His reckless behavior indicated that he could not (or did not) control his anger and he was dangerous. He was also a poor relationship risk. The risks included:

- Violent behavior (trying to throw her out of his car)
- Irresponsible behavior (not paying bills or child support)
- Spotty work history
- Uncontrolled emotional outbursts
- Alcohol abuse
- Inability to relate well to others (blaming)

- Previous failed intimate relationships
- Pattern of abuse and promises to do better

When we wrote his dysfunctional behaviors on a large chart, it was evident that they spelled trouble for the women in Sam's life. The first behavior, even if there were no others, was adequate reason to avoid Sam. Janet had believed Sam when he'd said, "I would never throw you from the car. I was drinking and I don't even remember doing it. I won't ever drink again. Please give me one more chance. You know that I love you." Every abused woman has heard this "I will be good" fairy tale. Janet no longer believes his promises, nor does she deny reality. Sam is dangerous. Janet decided that she could do better, and she was right.

In his excellent book, *The Gift of Fear* (1997), Gavin de Becker says that we "see" red flags that might protect us; yet we frequently ignore the warnings or explain them away: De Becker talks about violence:

> *I have learned some lessons about safety through years of asking people who have suffered violence, "Could you have seen this coming?" Most often they say, "No, it just came out of nowhere," but if I am quiet, if I wait a moment, here comes the information: "I felt uneasy when I first met this guy . . . " or "Now that I think of it, I was suspicious when he approached me" . . . Of course, if they realize it now, they knew it then. We all see the signals because there is a universal code of violence.*

If we are to stay safe from the predators in our midst, including intimate partners, we must learn to hear our internal alarm systems. We must also allow ourselves to respond appropriately to the alarm. It has taken millions of years of evolution to develop our amazing ability to "sense" danger. Let's use it wisely. I suggest that you read *The Gift of Fear*.

The Warning Signs of a Potential for Violence

In the literature, some characteristics are commonly linked to violent individuals. Five of the most consistent traits or behaviors are listed here. Watch for them. They are large flashing signals that say, "Take your time, slow down, and look for danger." As always, the best predictor of future behavior is past behavior.

- A history of violent or aggressive behavior
- Poor school performance
- A history of discipline problems or frequent run-ins with authority
- Uncontrolled anger
- Substance abuse

These warning signs are relatively obvious if they are recognized for what they are. However, a Psychopath or an Antisocial (these types are more likely to be violent than the average person), or someone who has these tendencies, can spin a very persuasive story. Poor school performance is explained by "I was so much more intelligent than the average student. I was bored." Discipline problems are the result of "the teachers had it in for me. I don't know why." Uncontrolled anger, of course, just is: "I have a bad temper like my old man. That is just the way I am." This is an attempt to transform uncontrolled anger into an inherited trait such as eye color or height.

More Warning Signs

Professionals at the University of Buffalo Counseling Center suggest paying close attention to what you hear and see when you are learning about a new person in your life. Remember, some individuals are very skilled at hiding their dark side.

Knowledge is your best protection. Take the time to get to know a man who interests you. This is a lengthy process, but it is well worth your time. Also, if you know something about his background, you have a better chance to perceive his "real" personality rather than a personality he chooses to project.

Buffalo Counseling Center Danger Warning Signs

- Emotionally abuses you (insults, belittling comments, ignores you, acts sulky or angry when you initiate an action or idea)
- Tells you who you may be friends with, how you should dress, or tries to control other elements of your life or relationship
- Talks negatively about women in general
- Gets jealous when there is no reason
- Drinks heavily, uses drugs, or tries to get you drunk
- Berates you for not wanting to get drunk, get high, have sex, or go with him to an isolated or personal place
- Refuses to let you share any of the expenses of a date and gets angry when you offer to pay
- Is physically violent to you or others, even if it's "just" grabbing and pushing to get his way
- Acts in an intimidating way toward you by invading your "personal space" (sits too close, speaks as if he knows you much better than he does, touches you when you tell him not to)
- Is unable to handle sexual and emotional frustrations without becoming angry
- Does not view you as an equal—because he's older or sees himself as smarter or socially superior
- Thinks poorly of himself and guards his masculinity by acting tough

- Goes through extreme highs and lows, is kind one minute and cruel the next
- Is angry and threatening to the extent that you have changed your life so as not to anger him

These behaviors indicate that the individual is bad mannered, disrespectful, self-centered, and obnoxious. Even if he did not have a potential for violence, walking away would make good sense.

Immediate Danger Signals

According to the American Psychological Association's Web site, these are the immediate warning signs that violence is a serious possibility. As we say in law enforcement, "He has the means; he only needs the opportunity." If you are in a relationship with a man who fits this pattern, it is time to make a safety plan, follow your plan, and get to safety. We will talk more about safety plans later in this chapter.

- Loss of temper on a daily basis
- Frequent physical fighting
- Significant vandalism or property damage
- Increased use of drugs or alcohol
- Increased risk-taking behavior
- Detailed plans to commit acts of violence
- Announces threats or plans for hurting others
- Enjoys hurting animals
- Carries a weapon

These indicators suggest that a violent incident may happen—soon. It is crucial that you recognize that the situation is spiraling down toward imminent danger. Listening carefully and responding to imminent danger is just as important as responding to warnings of a natural disaster, such as Hurricane Katrina. As we all know, especially those poor souls on the Gulf Coast, Katrina struck with catastrophic results as predicted. No matter what you may have heard to the contrary, predicting human behavior is much less complicated than predicting a force of nature.

Denial and Safety

Sometimes we see and understand the warning signs, yet we deny the meaning. We deny it because we don't want to be forced to act. If we say to ourselves, "Okay, I see the danger," then we have to act. We may be forced to leave a relationship we don't want to leave. Denial avoids this uncomfortable situation. The discomfort is called *cognitive dissonance*; it means our behavior is not consistent with what we believe. De Becker (1997) says of denial:

> *Denial has an interesting and insidious effect. For all the peace of mind deniers think they get by saying it isn't so, the fall they take when victimized is far, far greater than that of those who accept the possibility. Denial is a save-now-pay-later scheme, a contract written entirely in small print, for in the long run, the denying person knows the truth at some level, and it causes a constant low-grade anxiety.*

First, accept reality and then you are ready to plan for your future. Reality is seldom the way we would prefer it to be, but it is the only one we have.

A Safety Plan

Once we understand the conditions that spell danger, then we must act. Safety plans should be made in advance because the immediate situation might be chaotic. A safety plan should include such issues as:

- Where will I go?
- How will I get there?
- Whom do I need to call?
- What will I need to take with me?
- When should I leave?
- What should I say?

Where Will I Go?

A law enforcement officer, a victim's advocate, your attorney, or a rescue shelter volunteer can help you consider your options. Where you go depends on your particular situation. For some women, staying with friends or family is the best answer. If that is not possible, a women's shelter can be a safe environment, and the workers are experts at helping women in those circumstances. Many shelters provide a very comfortable and homelike atmosphere for women and their children.

How Will I Get There?

If you have the opportunity, you may be able to take your car. If not, you will need to decide who can pick you up or if public transportation is available. Safety is always the first consideration when making this decision. Again, a women's shelter or domestic abuse hot line may be the best possible resources for getting advice. They have been through this many times before.

Whom Do I Need to Call?

Whom do you tell that you are leaving? Possibly, you should tell your parents, siblings, a coworker, or a close friend that you are leaving, why you are leaving, and, if appropriate, where you will be living. Remember your mate will probably call people close to you in an attempt to find you.

What Will I Need to Take with Me?

Think carefully about this when making your plan. If you or a child takes medication, hide an extra supply somewhere. Depending on how much time you have, a few clothes would certainly make life easier. A favorite small toy can comfort a child in a strange new environment. Copies of your important papers would be helpful. Money, as much as you can save, comes in handy. Make an extra set of keys and hide them. You may need important telephone numbers and e-mail addresses. If you don't have a safe place to hide your necessities, leave them with someone you trust.

When Should I Leave?

You can probably predict when your mate will erupt. You have seen it happen before and you know the signs—trust your instinct. Also, review the Immediate Danger Signals in this chapter. As always, it is better to err on the side of caution.

What Should I Say?

Nothing should be left to chance. It is a good idea to have a code word that will alert your children when it is time to leave. They should know where to meet (i.e., in the backyard, in the garage) and what to take. Obviously, you will have already explained to them, according to their maturity level, why you are leaving and what they should do. Children want to be assured that someone who can handle the situation is in charge.

Always have a Plan B just in case Plan A doesn't work.

After You Leave

When you leave an abusive partner, you will need your support system. You may feel very alone and frightened, and that is perfectly normal. Spirituality can be extremely comforting now. Stay connected to the people you care about. Making life-changing decisions is neither easy nor painless. You may feel out of control, afloat, drifting in unfamiliar waters, but these feelings will pass in time. Your support system, your abuse advocate, your mental health professional, and your belief in yourself will keep you grounded.

What Is Being Done to Help Victims?

Our legal system and governments around the world are enacting antiviolence legislation in an attempt to stem the tide of partner abuse. This is heartening to hear, especially in countries such as India where the very fabric of the culture once condemned women to degradation and abuse. According to an article in the *Hindustan Times* (Singhvi, September 21, 2005):

> *The social context of India also justifies this kind of surgical legislative intervention (new anti abuse laws). One cannot forget that every six hours in India, a young married woman is burnt alive, beaten to death or driven to commit suicide. A recent study reports that at least 45 percent of Indian women are slapped, kicked or beaten by their husbands. There is an annual increase*

of 9.2 percent in cases of domestic violence, while a large number of cases go unreported.

This is a giant step forward for India and I applaud their commitment to protecting women. It will be interesting to follow this story and see if the new laws are energetically and uniformly enforced. In the United States, although laws were in place to protect all citizens from abuse, enforcement was spotty at best until recently. Now officers are required to arrest a batterer if the victim exhibits signs of physical abuse. Also, women no longer have to take responsibility for pressing charges. When women were required to press charges, it put them in a very awkward, if not dangerous, position. If they chose not to file, they were viewed as unmotivated by law enforcement. If they chose to file, they risked retribution by a hostile partner.

The Violence Against Women Act of 2000 (VAWA 2000) was a necessary step to put teeth in the laws protecting women, to conduct research, and to make services available to victims. Among other worthwhile expenditures, money is funneled into programs that assist victims (i.e., legal assistance, domestic abuse hot line) and research by the National Academy of Science to understand violence against women. If you would like to know more about this act, you can read the entire document on the U.S. Department of Justice's Web site.

A therapist can assist you in putting your life back together. Choose someone who has had experience working with women in abusive relationships.

Our choices create our present and our future. Choosing the right man with whom to share our lives is one of the most important choices we will ever make. There are "rules" to guide us in making an informed, intelligent, well-thought-out decision. Let's explore these rules in the next chapter.

CHAPTER 12

Why You Chose Mr. Wrong:
Making New Choices

When you choose your friends, don't be short-changed by choosing personality over character.
   W. Somerset Maugham

I ALWAYS ASK a female client why she chose her mate. What made him so special that she decided to spend the rest of her life with him? Why, out of the billions of available males on this planet, did he stand out as the "one and only." Many of these women are in unhealthy relationships. They want to be nudged in the right direction, and they want to believe there is a solution that will work for them. Frequently, they feel hopeless, out of control, and trapped. Yes, there are answers that we will talk about later, but they require effort, tenacity, the patience of Job, and a good support system. Nonetheless, we have the power to make healthy changes in our lives.

Please take a moment to make your own List A. Why did you choose the man in your life? The reasons for choosing Mr. Right usually fall into the following categories:

List A: Why I Was Attracted to My Mate
- Good looking
- Entertaining and exciting
- Flattering
- Charming
- Sexy

Would you be attracted to a man who had all of those attributes? Really? Superficially, he might be considered desirable. However, if you glance through our chapters on Psychopaths, Antisocials, and Narcissists, you will recognize these attributes as criteria symptoms. Yes, a Psychopath can be charming, sexy, exciting, and good looking, and he can also tune in on your dreams and fulfill them. He will tell you that you are wonderful, beautiful, and intelligent; your self-confidence will soar. Did you know that magicians used to use smoke and mirrors to obscure the audience's view and create illusions? Magicians were experts at the art of illusion, but no more so than the average manipulator. However, you have more at stake than a $5 entrance ticket. Never forget, Psychopaths, Antisocials, and Narcissists and their wannabe cousins are fully capable of winning the Pulitzer Prize for manipulation, improvisation, and deceit.

After looking at your List A, write down the characteristics and qualities you admire most in men. This is usually a little more difficult; it takes more thought and time. Your second list will probably include many of the following characteristics.

- Reliable
- Responsible
- Good-natured
- Honest
- Faithful
- Intelligent

- Compassionate
- Generous
- Emotionally mature
- Career oriented (but not a workaholic)
- Family oriented
- Spiritual
- Flexible
- Fair-minded
- Financially responsible

After you complete List B, go back to the first list and compare them. What do you discover? If the two lists of preferences are different, maybe we should explore the reasons. And as a friend brought to my attention, there is no reason that a man cannot win a Pulitzer Prize, be generous to a fault, *and* be Brendan Fraser–sexy with a fabulous sense of humor. Of course, I should mention that the line of woman waiting to meet him might circle the globe twice.

Most of us do not spend our leisure time wondering if that new hunk at work is honorable, principled, and reliable. However, when he doesn't show up for our first date, suddenly reliability, or rather his lack thereof, becomes our all-consuming focus.

The List B traits that are conducive to an enduring, mutually satisfying relationship are also the traits that are most vulnerable to neglect. Most of those character traits are not sexy or romantic; they don't sparkle or go from zero to sixty in 5.4 seconds. If we do think about them at all, it is because the exciting man we chose is pitifully devoid of them. If your List A is drastically different from your List B, there will be disappointments and painful gnashing of teeth.

Now you have the opportunity to consider your two lists. Perhaps you might want to consider List B a work–in–progress. It will probably change, and certainly lengthen, as you have time to mull over which characteristics have enhanced your relationships (i.e., kindness, compassion) and which ones have caused you pain (i.e., selfishness, dishonesty). Talking to your friends about their List B priorities could be very enlightening for all of you.

A loving, compassionate, honest, and trustworthy man is less likely to use manipulative behaviors than he is, suddenly and without warning, to huff and puff and blow your house down. These men are straightforward. You won't need a divining device to interpret their intentions or predict their future behavior. As always, past behavior is the best predictor of future behavior.

Isn't it wonderful to know you can have the best of both worlds? It takes many months to get to know a man. If you decide to probe the depth and breadth of his character, it may take years, or even a lifetime. Invest the time it takes to truly know if his generosity and compassion is genuine or simply a well-scripted part of the role he is playing. If you are objective, pay close attention, acknowledge the red flags, and refuse to distort unpleasant realities, he cannot deceive you.

Rule One: The truth is always consistent.

Are some women more vulnerable to the manipulative types than other women?

Who Is Vulnerable to Manipulation?

Anyone can be manipulated by a very skilled actor. Brad Pitt and Harrison Ford could consider themselves extremely fortunate if they had the extraordinary acting skills and talents of a manipulator with psychopathic and/or antisocial tendencies. Happily, we the prey can learn to understand the predators as well as they understand us. Most of this book has been dedicated to helping you travel inside the mind of a deceiver and "see" his method and goals rather than his elaborate smoke screen.

Some women are more vulnerable to deception than others. Manipulators can zoom in on a weakness or vulnerability in an incredibly brief time. Women who have been hurt before and are reluctant to trust can be deceived by an innocent and harmless façade. Such women may tell their friends: "He is the most wonderful man I've ever known. I feel safe telling him things I have never told anyone." Truthfully, he is a "wonderful man" when he chooses that role. "Wonderful" is a pretense he assumes and he can slip effortlessly into it, as if it were a cashmere coat. Be prepared, he is really the black leather jacket with silver studs. Be assured, there are great pretenders walking among us, and it is incredibly difficult to distinguish them from their more solid and genuine brothers. The pretenders are an alluring mirage that shimmers with promise, patiently waiting to seduce, deceive, and manipulate women who thirst for an intimate relationship. Manipulators play merciless, high-stake games with vulnerable women.

Predators are amazingly skillful observers; they have a primordial sixth sense for identifying women who have poor self-esteem and marginal self-confidence. The manipulator will flatter this kind of woman in the areas she feels least confident or competent. If the woman's belief system says, "I am unattractive" (you are not, because beauty has many faces), he will gush and eulogize her seductive bedroom eyes and extraordinary Barbie legs. His goal at the beginning of the relationship is to boost her self-confidence. He knows, and it is important that you also understand, we seek out and bond with individuals who "make" us feel good about ourselves.

Woman who are nurturers, who are champions of the disadvantaged underdogs of this world, are pathetically easy prey. They are trusting creatures; they have never developed healthy, self-protecting, suspicious minds. Manipulators toy with these women by occasionally stepping out of character and displaying the snarling wolf under the lamb's fleece. The manipulators are playing the adult version of peek-a-boo. A sinfully charming and pulse-racing, sexy manipulator told me, "I am hard to get to know and I am not worth it." He was absolutely right.

Manipulators are also exceptionally gifted liars. "Any fool can tell the truth," wrote British author Samuel Butler, "but it requires a man of some sense to know how to lie well." According to a recent study, lying requires more than just "some sense," it requires a unique brain. The distinctive brain of a liar may make lying easier. A University of Southern California study shows pathological liars have structural brain differences:

> *The theory that Yang and colleagues have developed is the extra connections between nerve cells give liars a greater ability to lie. Dr. Raine put it this way: "Lying takes a lot of effort." For example, "You have to be able to understand the mindset of the other person (and) to suppress your emotions or regulate them because you don't want to appear nervous (Michael Smith, MedPage Today).*

If a genuine thought should escape the manipulator's mouth, he will deny it, saying either, "You misunderstood me or I am tired, hungry, or drunk." Take your choice. As Lord Byron noted, "And, after all, what is a lie? 'Tis but the truth in masquerade." Manipulators enjoy entertaining cat-and-mouse games. Machiavellian amusements feed their exaggerated egos. Refuse to be a mouse.

Women who believe that they have few romantic options ignore red flags. They earnestly want to believe in him. They resist accepting reality; the entire world is a stage and he is an accomplished actor. Once the manipulator feels secure, the "good guy" role rides off into the sunset and he reverts to Mr. Hyde. He can be in jolly spirits when it suits his purpose and detestable if he is bored, contradicted, criticized, or opposed.

The Qualities of a Healthy Relationship

Ted Huston, a professor at the University of Texas at Austin, has studied intimate relationships for thirty years. He began a longitudinal study of couples in 1979 and followed those couples for fourteen years. He hoped to discover the differences between happy marriages that grow and mature and marriages that deteriorate and end in divorce. His study found some of the qualities we have been discussing. Here are the qualities he found in healthy marriages (be sure to add them to your list).

Marriages in which one or both spouses possess stereotypically "feminine" traits such as warmth, kindness, and a high level of concern for others tend to evidence a strong degree of marital satisfaction and are preceded by courtships that show a smooth, even progression toward marriage. Individuals with so-called feminine traits typically behave more affectionately and elicit similar behavior from a partner, and they are inclined to give each other the benefit of the doubt.

Warmth, kindness, and a high level of concern are qualities we all enjoy. A friend recently told me that her husband was never protective of her. "Not protective" meant he was not particularly concerned about her safety, her needs, or her self-esteem. Affection (i.e., hugging, kissing, and holding hands) is definitely on my "want" list. Numerous studies have suggested that human touch is essential for good health.

Rice University: Qualities of a Good Marriage

The Rice University Relationship page discusses qualities of a good relationship. *Respect* is important to the success of any human interaction. A veteran police officer told me that he learned early in his career to be respectful of everyone, including suspects. He believes that is the reason he has never had to unholster his gun. Respect should be a given in an intimate relationship. *Trust* is the glue that bonds lovers together. If unfounded suspicion is introduced into a viable relationship, it will erode that bond. *Honesty* is the foundation on which trust is built. It is better to be scrupulously honest (not blunt or hurtful) even when honesty carries a price tag.

How often do you hear the words: *That's not fair.* I hear them quite often. Humans appear to have an innate scale for measuring fairness. If you have fairness, it means using objective evidence to determine what works for your mate and for you. Neither of you will be right or wrong all of the time. In fact, *right* and *wrong* are abstract concepts, and as such, they are impossible to substantiate. Fairness means giving as well as receiving—in equal measure.

Transforming Abstract Concepts into Behaviors

Concept: I am "right."
John, you should be more loving.

Behaviors: What works for us.
John, I really enjoy sitting on the sofa and holding your hand while we watch television.

As you know, a concept such as *loving* is open to interpretation. However, when *loving* is translated into a behavior (i.e., holding hands), it becomes something we all understand and can, if motivated, perform acceptably.

If both you and your partner take *responsibility* for the success of your relationship, it has an excellent chance of being just that—successful. All couples have mundane tasks that must be accomplished. If each partner accepts responsibility for his or her share of the tasks (i.e., taking out the trash, feeding the dog, buying groceries), you can avoid hoarding trivial grievances until they overwhelm and suffocate your relationship. Taken individually, these grievances are insignificant; if they become an established pattern, they move from insignificant to exceptionally annoying. No doubt, you have noticed that manipulators are not conscientious and they are not team players. Many manipulations are calculated to defer responsibility. Again, lofty promises serve as a distraction and a smoke screen. If your partner's behaviors do not change accordingly, his words are hollow and meaningless.

When we are young and more pliable, one of our life tasks is to mature as a responsible adult. Many adults have never internalized this life task and, in fact, aggressively avoid assuming responsibility for their actions or their relationships. Author and philosopher Phillip Atkinson explores the early years in which manipulators fine-tune and perfect their manipulative skills:

> *For it was by fooling parental authority that they learnt how to indulge their wants while avoiding penalty for their crimes. The instinctive children's tears to deter wrath; pretence of sickness to win sympathy; lies to avert justice; all become dependable tools to regularly employ. To win their own way they know what expressions to adopt, what words to utter and what tone to invoke.*

Unambiguous *communication* helps to sidestep other potential dangers. Frequently, a troubled spouse listens to his partner, and then interprets her words in accordance with his antagonistic "circle the wagons" belief system. He then transforms all of her communication into criticism or a demeaning indictment. An effective way to avoid verbal misunderstandings is to repeat what we "hear" and then ask for clarification if we are unsure what is meant. To the detriment of marriages, what we "hear" and what is said (and meant) can be poles apart.

According to research, happy couples normally have these healthy qualities: respect, trust, honesty, fairness, responsibility, and good communication. If you and your partner have them, I commend you. If you don't, then you know where to concentrate your effort and energy. If you are not in a relationship and are contemplating your mate options, these couple-friendly qualities can be a point of reference by which you measure prospective mates.

Resilience: What It Means and How It Helps

If you have been in a dysfunctional relationship with a manipulative man, you probably have emotional wounds you long to heal. In fact, simply living our lives can be a wounding experience. Life regularly challenges us emotionally, psychologically, and physically. Learning to be more resilient can fill the potholes, take out some of the sharp curves, and smooth the road to recovery. If you are still in a dysfunctional relationship, resilience may be just what you need to walk away with confidence (while singing "I Will Survive"), knowing that you can thrive without him.

Resilience is the ability to take the cream pies that life throws at you and enjoy them with a cup of robust coffee. Resilience means coping with adversity in a healthy and adaptive manner. You are healthy if you have few stress symptoms after you are challenged by misfortune. Adaptive means that you learn from your daunting experiences and grow as a person. A stressor could be a tense, unhealthy job environment; a conflicted relationship; losing someone you love through death; serious illness; or the dissolution of a valued intimate relationship. Demanding situations are certainly not rare; they come along with annoying regularity. I often hear clients say, "This is terrible. I have the worst luck. I didn't need this." Resilience is the ability to remain positive, or at least neutral, when the rain is coming in through the roof and you just used the last pot in the house to catch the latest drip. Resilient people bounce back and land on their feet and say, "Wow! I sure am glad I had enough pots." They don't have fewer "bad hair days" than anyone else; they simply handle them better.

Resilience is often found in individuals we might consider fragile. For example, the elderly can withstand emotional upheaval and survive with fewer scars than their juniors. Disaster survivors are an excellent example:

> *Hurricane Katrina seemed to single out the elderly for particular punishment—people such as 86-year-old Pearline Chambers. She spent two days alone in her one-story house in the submerged Ninth Ward of New Orleans, with hurricane floodwater up to her neck. She lost her false teeth, her wig and her cats. "I just waded around and waded around, trying to get up in my attic," said Chambers, a widow. "I kept climbing and slipping and falling in that water." Two weeks after the storm, though, Chambers feels fine. Living now with her sister's family, she said she has nobody but "my stubborn self" to blame for ignoring hurricane warnings and refusing to flee New Orleans . . . (Washington Post, September 14, 2005).*

If you are in a relationship with a manipulative man, then much like Pearline Chambers, you have weathered stormy days. You may sometimes feel as if you are living in a hurricane or going crazy. Manipulation is meant to control your behavior. When we feel out of control, it can seem as if we are losing our minds. I have felt the same way when I counseled someone with a personality disorder.

Resilience is often the product of surviving difficult, emotionally demanding situations, and internalizing the knowledge that you can, have, and will prevail. Stress is created when a person doubts his or her resources (internal and external) and capability to overcome adversity. Fortunately, resilience can be strengthened and empowered.

The Resiliency Test

How resilient are you? Take the test. Mark your answer to each statement by indicating either *yes, sometimes,* or *no.*

1. I can think of various solutions for problems.
   Yes ○   Sometimes ○   No ○

2. I have a sense of humor and can laugh at myself and at life.
   Yes ○   Sometimes ○   No ○

3. I bounce back quickly from stressful situations.
   Yes ○   Sometimes ○   No ○

4. I allow myself to lean on my support system as needed.
   Yes ○   Sometimes ○   No ○

5. My outlook on life is positive; the glass is half full and more is coming.
   Yes ○   Sometimes ○   No ○

6. I feel comfortable expressing my feelings.
   Yes ○   Sometimes ○   No ○

7. I work out at least three times a week.
   Yes ○   Sometimes ○   No ○

8. I eat regular healthful meals.
   Yes ○   Sometimes ○   No ○

9. I regularly use meditation, yoga, or relaxation/guided imagery to relax.
   Yes ○   Sometimes ○   No ○

10. I feel that I have achieved balance in all areas of my life.
    Yes ○   Sometimes ○   No ○

11. I avoid overdosing on sugar, fat, and caffeine.
    Yes ○   Sometimes ○   No ○

12. I find ways to have fun while going about my daily activities.
    Yes ○   Sometimes ○   No ○

13. I plan at least one "fun, let's enjoy life" activity each week.
    Yes ○   Sometimes ○   No ○

14. People have commented that I seem laid-back.
    Yes ○   Sometimes ○   No ○

15. I feel an inner peace that helps me in times of stress.
    Yes ○   Sometimes ○   No ○

16. My good opinion of myself is not dependent on others.
    Yes ○   Sometimes ○   No ○

17. I have an active spiritual life.
    Yes ○   Sometimes ○   No ○

18. I freely give hugs to the people I care about.
    Yes ○   Sometimes ○   No ○

19. I use logic to solve problems.
    Yes ○   Sometimes ○   No ○

20. I am inquisitive and enjoy learning.
    Yes ○   Sometimes ○   No ○

21. I am flexible.
    Yes ○   Sometimes ○   No ○

22. I am independent, yet I can work well with others.
    Yes ○   Sometimes ○   No ○

23. I have learned from my mistakes and my triumphs.
    YES ○   SOMETIMES ○   No ○

24. I don't feel overwhelmed with regret or guilt.
    YES ○   SOMETIMES ○   No ○

25. I am a natural leader (people look to me for leadership).
    YES ○   SOMETIMES ○   No ○

26. I remain calm and can continue to function well when faced with an emergency.
    YES ○   SOMETIMES ○   No ○

First, let me say, no matter what your score, we are all resilient. Some individuals are more resilient than others. Your score will indicate the general range of your resilience. We already know that you are inquisitive, are a problem solver, use logic, and are an independent thinker—otherwise you would not be reading the book and taking the test. Good for you!

Scoring the Test

Give yourself two points for each *sometimes*, three points for each *yes*, and zero points for each *no*. Add your scores.

Scores 0 to 25

Your resilience, according to your score, is in the marginal to moderate level. Either you are at the lower end of the resilience continuum or you were a little too hard on yourself. Measurement tests of this type are merely indicators; the individual scores have little meaning. Whatever your score happens to be, you are attempting to make a difference in your life and I think you should get an extra twenty points for reading the book and taking the test. Since I wrote the test and developed the scoring, I have the power to give you those twenty points. Congratulations! Now, let me suggest that you look at each one of your no answers and work on those particular areas. Ask friends and family members for their opinion; your scoring may be inaccurate. Trying to see ourselves as we really are is fraught with danger. Asking for objective feedback is always a good idea.

Scores 26 to 60

You scored in the middle-moderate to moderate-high level. Again, individual scores have little meaning except for indicating the range in which your score falls. We know you have many traits that are common in individuals who are resilient. Good for you! As with the last group, I suggest that you look at your no answers and get objective feedback from your support group. After you have determined the areas in which you could improve, begin the improvement process. There are many resources available to help you make changes; so, go forth and conquer.

Most readers will fall into this group.

Scores 61 to 78

Well done! It appears that you are at the higher end of the continuum. However, unless you scored 78, there is still work to be done. Keep in touch and let me know how you progress.

How Resilience Can Help You Overcome Manipulation

Winston Churchill said, "An appeaser is one who feeds a crocodile—hoping it will eat him last." Realize that you will never please a manipulator; they are insatiable. Here is where resilience comes in. Ask yourself why you appease? Is it because you love this man and you want to meet his every wish and desire? Although that is certainly a laudable goal, especially if he is someone who deserves it, regrettably it is impossible. We cannot meet someone's every wish, nor should we try. Each of us is responsible for his or her happiness. If your partner were a manipulator, it would be in his best interest to ask directly for what he wants rather than using deception.

Resilience allows you to say no clearly and forcefully without feeling that you must offer explanations. It will also allow you to accept a disagreeable response from your manipulator without feeling intimidated. After all, you know that you are in control of your life and your opinion is the one that counts. If you refuse to play the game, he will either stop manipulating or find someone who is willing to play the game. If he has been abusive in the past or you have reason to believe that he might become abusive if you confront him—be very cautious. Never take a chance with your safety. Please reread Chapter 11 on safety plans.

Increasing Resilience

A new theory called "positive psychology" is gaining acceptance. The proponents advocate accentuating the positives in our lives. Though this theory is called "new," it has been a focus of therapy for quite some time. I have always believed and counseled that we use our strengths to build more adaptive behaviors and beliefs. Our strengths include all of our internal and external resources.

Psychologist Barbara Fredrickson is a positive psychology advocate. In a recent study, Dr. Fredrickson and colleagues found that looking for and noting one's positives on a daily basis did "increase positive emotions, did increase resilience, and led to lower levels of depression, compared to a group of students who did not note the positive meaning they found in their experiences" (Albernaz, *Science & Spirit*).

Recent work with exploring gratitude and forgiveness as well as contentment and amusement seems to indicate that concentrating on these life tasks has a beneficial effect on our emotional and physical well-being. Alcoholics Anonymous has included forgiveness work as part of their program since the 1930s. Obviously, letting go of problematic emotional baggage frees energy that can be used in a more beneficial way.

Professor Bruce Smith of the University of New Mexico is interested in the factors that promote resilience, positive adaptation, and good health. He suggests that these factors are " . . . emotion regulation, emotional disclosure, gratitude, meaning and purpose, mindfulness meditation, spirituality and religion, and finding benefits or posttraumatic growth" (*http://pysch .unm.edu*). Regulating our emotions has a cycling effect. When we calm ourselves, we feel competent and in control, which is calming as well. From this, we learn that we have the ability to cope well in emotionally charged situations. Learning that we are resilient actually increases our conscious resilience and self-confidence.

Let's go back to Pearline Chambers, the senior hurricane survivor. After reading the newspaper article, we can risk certain assumptions. It is likely that she learned through life experiences that she should *persevere* (she kept attempting to climb into her attic) and that she had the *ability* to persevere. A mere two weeks after the hurricane, Ms. Chambers reports feeling "fine." She was able to *bounce back* from her ordeal. She is now living with her family on higher ground. Therefore, we can presume that she *accepts assistance* from her support system. She experienced two major stressors: the storm and the need to move away from her home. According to the newspaper article, "she lost her false teeth, her wig and her cats." Yet, she was able to look back at her experience and *take responsibility* for her decisions. She said she has nobody but "my stubborn self" to blame for ignoring hurricane warnings and refusing to flee New Orleans. In accepting responsibility, Ms. Chambers, a truly remarkable woman, also acknowledged the *power* and control she has in her life.

Resilience Factors

The good news is that it is possible to enhance our resilience, and research indicates that the following behaviors, beliefs, and attitudes will help:

- Ability to bounce back
- Accepting assistance from one's support system
- Accepting responsibility for one's decisions (which is not the same as blaming)
- Perseverance
- Acknowledging one's personal power
- Experiencing challenging situations and coping well
- Regulating emotions
- Disclosing emotions
- Showing gratitude
- Forgiveness
- Enjoying and acknowledging the positives in life (i.e., amusement)
- Contentment
- Spirituality
- Meaning and purpose
- Finding benefits in distressing situations

This, of course, is not an exhaustive list. Start anywhere on the list, add some of your own, and work toward exceptional self-confidence and competence. There is a strong negative correlation between genuinely appreciating yourself and not allowing anyone to misuse you. In other words, as your "I like me" index goes up, the misuse you will tolerate plummets.

How can you become more resilient? Learn to forgive, which does not mean that you must or should condone. Find the benefits in your darkest life experiences, even if the benefit is simply surviving it—that is a strength. Search for spirituality; you will find what you are looking for. Discover contentment in your life. This is the philosophy of a content individual, as described by Paul Wong, Ph.D.

> *They are able to forgive all those who have hurt them, even without any apology from their abusers.*
>
> *They are happy with what they have and who they are, but also strive to fulfill their potentials and responsibilities.*
>
> *They accept their place in the world, and yet they strive to overcome obstacles and pursue their calling.*

What more could we ask than the opportunity to fulfill our potential? You have certainly overcome obstacles. The focus is on you, not on your mate. Your choices will determine the life you live and with whom you share that unique gift. You have the power to create a life that reflects who you are and what is important to you. Your spirit cannot be manipulated nor can it be controlled.

Remember, you only have as much control in your relationship as your mate will give to you. You have complete control over your behavior and more control than you realize over your emotions and thoughts.

Since you can control you, why not start now? We have today, but we cannot be certain of anything beyond that point. A sense of control is calming, so take control over those elements of life that you can control: your thoughts, your reactions, and your behaviors. Healthy decisions affect your physical well-being as well as your perceived emotional well-being. You know how to be healthy: Eat more fruits and vegetables, exercise each day, eat lean meats and fish, enjoy an adequate support system, and learn and use relaxation techniques (such as deep breathing, yoga, meditation, relaxation/guided imagery, biofeedback). A healthy body copes with stress at optimal levels. Besides, healthy is beautiful.

CHAPTER 13

Don't Fall into the
Manipulation Trap

Me, I'm dishonest, and you can always trust a dishonest man to be dishonest. Honestly, it's the honest ones you have to watch out for.
⟨ *Johnny Depp*

MANIPULATION IS A CONTAGIOUS DISEASE, much more dangerous than the flu because it can endure for a lifetime. If you live with a manipulative man you don't have to worry about his artful ploys to control your behavior. You will know how to identify them after reading this book. Once you recognize manipulation for what it really is, it loses all power to influence you. The true danger is in acquiring your mate's disease and using manipulation as an inoculation against his dishonest and unfair tactics.

What if you also grew up in a family in which manipulation reined as the coping technique of choice? If you were not taught to be assertive, honest, and straightforward you would not have understood your man's manipulation as the insidious ploy that it was. Now you understand. No matter, if you learned manipulation long ago, or simply caught it when your mate sneezed, it is limiting your life in some fundamental ways. Intimate relationships are built on a foundation of "knowing" your partner. The definition of knowing is, "possessing knowledge, information, or understanding" and "suggestive of secret or private knowledge."

You do not "know" a manipulative man; he has worked diligently at spinning a web of contradictions, confusion, and falsehoods. Without knowing him you cannot trust him to be truthful or consistent, and most manipulations have an element of verbal dishonesty. You might be reluctant to be vulnerable with him. Perhaps you don't feel safe enough to share your tender emotions. Have you ever wondered if he might wield them as a weapon if you did?

This may also be true in your relationships with friends and family. When you communicate assertively there are no doubts about who you "really" are or where you stand on any issue. A manipulative woman remains a stranger in all of her relationships. Manipulation, much like anger, serves a purpose, it creates and maintains distance.

How do you know if you are manipulating? Try the following beliefs and behaviors on for size. If one resonates with you, you may want to give it some thought. If several apply, you need to control your environment to feel at peace. There are healthy, adaptive alternatives to controlling beliefs and behaviors. Let me suggest that you try some of the alternatives and see how they feel to you.

Control Beliefs and Traits: Healthy Alternatives

Manipulative individuals normally have a high need to control their lives, situations, and the people in their lives. Do these beliefs and traits sound familiar to you?

You are fearful and distrustful of others' intentions

EXAMPLE: "I bet they would take advantage of me with half a chance. You can't trust people."

ALTERNATIVE: A trusting nature with a dose of healthy skepticism until you "know" someone.

EXAMPLE: "Most people are trustworthy. However, I am cautious about forming a relationship with a man until I know something about him."

You anticipate others' emotions and respond accordingly to keep life's boat steady

EXAMPLE: "I can tell that working on the sink is beginning to annoy Jim. I had better stay out of sight. Gosh, my heart is starting to beat fast."

ALTERNATIVE: Your emotions are based on what is happening to you, not on the constantly changing moods of people in your life. For example, your mate is melancholy because it is raining. His melancholia and the rain do not necessitate an emotional response from you. Boats will rock and that is okay.

EXAMPLE: "Jim is trying to fix the sink. I hope he can fix it."

You attempt to fix the wounded birds in life

EXAMPLE: David can't pay his rent. I'm his big sister. I'll help him.

ALTERNATIVE: You may certainly choose to help birds without taking full responsibility for their welfare. It can become quite an emotional burden. Taking care of you is always worthwhile.

EXAMPLE: "David can't pay his rent. It's unfortunate that he chose to spent his rent money on other things."

In your relationships you believe you are capable of (and responsible for) fixing any problems

EXAMPLE: "Jim and I argue about bills and he gets very upset. I must think of a way to make more money."

ALTERNATIVE: You can fix your part of the problem and encourage the other person. Then let him decide what he is willing to invest in the relationship.

EXAMPLE: "Jim and I argue about bills. I think I will encourage him to discuss the problem with me. Working together, we can find a solution."

You accept responsibility for things over which you have no power (an impossible position)

EXAMPLE: "Jim is forty pounds overweight. I'll change his diet and ask him what he eats each day to be sure he isn't cheating."

ALTERNATIVE: Ask yourself before you mount your steed and ride to the rescue, "Do I have the power to change this situation? If I do have the power, "Is it my responsibility?" If either answer is a resounding "no" consider allowing whoever has the power and responsibility to fix the problem.

EXAMPLE: "Jim is forty pounds overweight. If he decides to lose weight, I'll be very proud of him. I really should eat more healthful foods."

You like order in your life, if people you care about are left to their own devices they might run amuck; you jump in to help them

EXAMPLE: "This is Heather's last year in high school and her grades are dismal. If I talk to her teachers and supervise her homework assignments she might pull her grades up."

ALTERNATIVE: Again, decide if you have the power and responsibility. Unless, the person involved is your child (a young child), you are not responsible. People have and will run amuck at times; it relieves the tedium. It is perfectly okay to sit back and enjoy a cup of tea until they resolve their issue. You don't have to earn worth, you are already worthy.

EXAMPLE: "This is Heather's last year in high school and her grades are dismal. I hope she chooses to spend more time studying. I'll encourage her efforts."

You are in a nurturing profession to heal your family or self

EXAMPLE: "I can fix my family of origin. I have the counseling skills to facilitate healthy adaptive behaviors."

ALTERNATIVE: Individuals from dysfunctional families frequently join one of the nurturing professions to work out their family problems or renew their role as a care taker. That isn't bad, however it should be recognized. You cannot "save" your family and you cannot "save" the world. You can contribute by being assertive, compassionate, and interested in your fellow man.

EXAMPLE: "I know I can't fix mom and dad, but I can model healthy, adaptive behaviors."

You find it difficult to delegate

EXAMPLE: "Wow! There is so much work to do. If I work late every night this week I might be able to catch up."

ALTERNATIVE: It is perfectly acceptable to say, "I need your help on this project." Trying to do everything yourself is a heavy burden. If you find that you have more tasks than time . . . try delegating. If you hear the word "no," that is acceptable also and you will be no worse off than before you asked.

EXAMPLE: "Wow! We have so much work to do. Okay guys, how do you think we should handle this?"

If you had been on the Titanic you would have taken charge of a lifeboat and probably rowed it all the way to New York

EXAMPLE: "Darn, it is cold out here! Move out of the way, I'll save you, I am rowing to New York."

ALTERNATIVE: It is very unlikely that you are completely alone without seaworthy help. Let them help you to row . . . ask, if they do not volunteer. You will get there faster and not be as exhausted. Also, working together connects us with other people. I love win-win situations.

EXAMPLE: "Darn, it's cold out here! I'll help with the rowing."

Do you have difficulty accepting change?

EXAMPLE: "My job has been eliminated! I don't know what to do! This is terrible and I can't stand it!"

ALTERNATIVE: Individuals who grew up in chaotic homes may fear change. They want stability and quiet. Change is okay; it is the only thing on which we can depend. You can tell yourself change is inevitable and you can enjoy the adventure. Take it one step at a time and consider the opportunities it creates.

EXAMPLE: "My job has been eliminated! I will have to give this some thought and talk with friends. I might go back to school. It will be scary for awhile, but I'll survive."

Do you react with more emotion than your friends or coworkers when life's little crises happen?

EXAMPLE: "The photocopier isn't working! I have all these copies to make (wiping cold sweat from brow). I don't know what I will do!"

ALTERNATIVE: We sometimes upset ourselves when a crisis occurs because we tell ourselves we cannot handle it. Take a deep breath, look for the resources you need to conquer the crisis and form your plan of action. Once you have a viable plan you will feel in control. Again, ask yourself, "Is this my responsibility?" before you attack.

EXAMPLE: "The photocopier isn't working? I think I'll catch up on some computer work. Let me know when it is fixed."

Do you draw in others to support your position in a dispute?

EXAMPLE: "Mr. Morgan, I hate to bother you, but Susan is being so snippy, all of the assistants are threatening to look for other jobs."

ALTERNATIVE: Talk to the person with whom you have the dispute. You are the only two individuals who can resolve it. If he refuses to participate then accept that a resolution is impossible. Pulling children into adult conflicts is especially harmful.

EXAMPLE: "Susan, I would like to talk with you. Are you okay? Is something bothering you?"

If several of the indicators apply to you, you have a tendency to control. Remember, a tendency to control is not like a tendency to rob banks. It is neither good nor bad, it simply *is*. Interestingly, one could say that Mother Teresa had a control issue using these criteria. Yet, the Catholic Church is considering sainthood for the venerable nun. Most successful people take charge of situations and anyone standing close. If you attempt to control situations over which you have control and your attempt makes life better (without harming anyone), then it is healthy. However, if your efforts are focused on other people or uncontrollable circumstances, then you may feel frustrated and powerless.

Would you like to know more about manipulative behaviors? Read on.

Manipulative Behaviors and Assertive Alternatives

These are common manipulative behaviors. Do you use any of them to influence others? What could you do instead that would be assertive and healthy for you *and* your relationship?

Do you attempt (using a ruse) to pull individuals back into your circle if they are emotionally moving away?

ASSERTIVE ALTERNATIVE: Tell him you have noticed a distance growing in your relationship and ask if he would like to talk about it. It is certainly okay to say, "Your friendship is valuable to me and I would be sad if I lost it." If he refuses to acknowledge the distance and walks away, that is his right. We don't own friends, they come and go. Though losing a friend is sad, we can and do survive without him.

Do you minimize your abilities and strengths to gain rescuers?

ASSERTIVE ALTERNATIVE: You may have learned that you needed to be dependent to gain support and at one time that may have been true. However, most people are drawn to someone who is independent and capable of handling life's challenges. It is okay to show the strong and competent person you are.

Do you use guilt to gain cooperation from family or friends?

ASSERTIVE ALTERNATIVE: Guilt is certainly a potent motivator; however it wears thin pretty quickly. Attempt asking for what you need and want in a straightforward, concise way. You are very likely to get it and you will also gain respect.

Do you promise cooperation to achieve a goal and then renege?

ASSERTIVE ALTERNATIVE: Be careful when you make a promise. If you don't think you can keep it, then promise something you will do. Or just say, "I hope I can do this, but it is not entirely under my control. I will do my best." Promises not kept undermine respect and credibility.

Do you threaten to abandon your significant other to gain cooperation?

ASSERTIVE ALTERNATIVE: One, this doesn't work. He learns very quickly that it is something you say, not something you do. Two, eventually he will say, "Okay, go ahead and leave." What would you do then? Draw a line in the sand, tell him what you will do, choose something reasonable, and follow through. He will respect your resolve and strength, though he may not change.

Do you play on others' desire to help or feel important?

ASSERTIVE ALTERNATIVE: Simply ask for whatever you want or need. Compliments and approval feel good and should be sprinkled in your conversation if they are genuine. Insincere compliments have no value and people see through them.

Do you use your anger to intimidate?

ASSERTIVE ALTERNATIVE: Though intimidation sometimes works, it also creates distance and alienates people. Be straightforward and calmly state your case. If he gets angry, walk away until tempers cool. Nothing worthwhile is accomplished in anger. Intimidating people are not liked or respected, they are feared.

Do you feel entitled and ask for more attention than you give?

ASSERTIVE ALTERNATIVE: We all enjoy positive attention. However, it is not our God-given right. You don't have to be the center of attention to be okay. Try standing back and just watching for awhile, you may decide that you like it.

Do you blame others for your mistakes?

ASSERTIVE ALTERNATIVE: As Colette said, "You will do foolish things, but do them with enthusiasm." We are not our mistakes. We are so much more. One mistake, no matter how grievous it may appear at the time, is no more than a grain of sand on the beach of life. Take a deep breath, throw out your chest, hold your head high and say, "Yes, I did that. It was *my* mistake." The prouder you sound the more it will confuse people.

Do you lie to achieve goals or calm choppy waters?

ASSERTIVE ALTERNATIVE: This one is easy, tell the truth or simply say nothing. Once you are caught in a lie (and you will be caught) you have lost someone's trust. I know that it can become a habit and you do it without thinking, especially if you grew up in a harsh family. Stop and think a moment before you speak.

Do you tell people what they want to hear to make them like you?

ASSERTIVE ALTERNATIVE: It is very possible that they will like you anyway. If not, there are people who will. We aren't going to please everyone . . . it is impossible. It is okay to have an honest disagreement. Try saying what you really think (within reason) and see what happens. You may see a new respect in their eyes. You may even like yourself more.

Do you cling to your significant other as if you were about to drown?

ASSERTIVE ALTERNATIVE: Are you underestimating your ability? When you were a small child you were truly helpless. You are now a capable adult. I have found that the more we cling, the more mates pull away. Ask yourself, "Could I survive without him?" You survived before you met him *and* there are 6.2 billion people on this earth (half of which are male). Learn to value the unique woman you are, he will value you more also.

I have noticed that a mate runs if you attempt to smother him. If the smothering behavior stops, he turns around, notices you are not a step behind and draws closer to you. I cannot promise that your partner will respond in this way. Nonetheless, I frequently observe this reversal of roles in counseling.

Do you act ill to gain nurturing?

ASSERTIVE ALTERNATIVE: Ask for what you need rather than putting yourself through the drama of pretending to be ill. Possibly, at an early age, you were shown parental concern and attention when you were ill and attention was underprovided at other times. Are the people in your life nurturing? Why not give them the chance to prove they are by asking them for attention? At times you may need to nurture yourself with a steamy, bubbly bath, or a stroll in a beautiful setting. Perhaps trying something new, such as yoga, would be helpful. Reading a new book by one of my favorite authors lifts my spirits.

Do you frequently agree with people just to avoid conflict?

ASSERTIVE ALTERNATIVE: At times this is not a bad idea, especially if you can genuinely agree with something they are expressing. However, it doesn't work well as a central coping skill. What's the problem? You are not being yourself, you have to pretend to believe and feel differently than you actually do. You might begin to wonder who you really are. You cannot avoid conflict; it is inevitable, so express *yourself*. It will feel slightly uncomfortable at first, but you will soon learn to enjoy the satisfaction that comes from expressing your distinctive perspective.

Do you "choose" emotions (i.e., sad, angry) when it helps you to achieve a goal?

ASSERTIVE ALTERNATIVE: Emotions are very powerful elements of our communication. Express the emotions you feel without wondering what will work. Human beings are perceptive; they will pick up on the masquerade, especially if they know you well, such as a significant other. If you don't think you should show honest emotions, ask yourself, "Why not?" Insincere emotional responses are another way to lose credibility. Extreme emotions will frighten or alienate people. Mild to moderate are normally accepted well.

Do you feel powerful? Let's talk about power.

Internal and External Power

If we believe that we are powerful, we have no need to control or manipulate others. We want to have the power to set goals and reach those goals. Our perceived power may be distinctly different from our actual power. If you believe you are in control of your life, then you are in control. A recent study indicated that men who *thought* they were physically fit, were more likely to be healthy than men who *thought* they were not. In reality, there may have been no physical differences in the men; a positive perception of reality is healthy. The study underscored the importance of believing in yourself and maintaining an optimistic outlook. The test subjects had the power to exercise (which all of them did) and they had the power to perceive themselves through an affirming lens.

Internal Power

In my professional opinion, developed over my fifteen years of counseling experience, there are six variables that contribute to your internal power. Internal power is the power you ascribe to yourself. If you say to yourself, "I am powerful, a force with which to be reckoned (and believe it)" others will also perceive you as powerful. Power is not about size or physical strength; it is about an all abiding belief in you and your ability to shape your world. The six variables are: Inner peace, courage, forgiveness and letting go, sharing love and wellness.

Let's learn about the power variables.

Inner peace

Inner peace is an internal balance that cannot be tilted by others' words or deeds. Inner peace is created by meditating, practicing relaxation/guided imagery or yoga. Calming meditations teach your body to relax and focus your energy inward. In order to do this you must temporarily shut out the external world. I suggest designating a space in your home, ideally a room, or even a small corner, to be used for relaxation and focusing. This space should have whatever you need to concentrate, relax, and feel safe and contented. Some common elements are soothing colors, soft music, comfortable furniture, soft pillows and your personal "feel good" objects.

How will you know when you have achieved inner peace? Watch for these symptoms: spontaneity, unprecedented joy, enhanced creativity, pleasure in simple things, a healthy acceptance of your strengths and limitations, an overwhelming desire to smile, a yearning to share and an eagerness to grow and experience.

Good news! When you find and cultivate your inner serenity and peace, your mate will no longer have the power to push your buttons.

Courage

Courage is needed to make changes in your life. It takes courage to accept yourself as you are, though you may want to grow. Growth follows acceptance. It takes courage to examine your relationship with your mate and decide if it meets your needs or can be changed to meet your needs. It takes courage to set ambitious goals and go after them. It takes courage to face the past. As Maya Angelou said, "History, despite its wrenching pain, cannot be unlived, but if faced with courage, need not be lived again."

You have courage; it comes as standard equipment at no additional charge. Ask yourself, "When have I been courageous?" If you don't have an answer, ask someone who loves you.

Forgiveness and Letting Go

Emotional baggage is a fact of life. We all have it. Emotional baggage is no more than strong negative emotion that ties us to someone or something in our past. Forgiving is one way to cut the emotional ties. Hate, fear, and anger are exceptionally strong tethers; they keep us attached to the painful periods and people we struggle to leave behind. Forgiving does not mean condoning. Forgiving says, "I don't want you in my heart or my mind ever again. You must go now. Go in peace." If you discover that letting go or forgiving is depleting your energy, consult a therapist. He or she can help you free yourself from your past's clinging web.

As one of my favorite authors, Oscar Wilde, said, "Always forgive your enemies—nothing annoys them so much."

Accepting Your Power

You must accept your power and detect it working in your daily life. Power is quiet, it seldom says something twice, it expects to be heard and it can be remarkably gentle. Some people, especially the aggressive and abusive, believe that power is a big stick wielded to control the weak. Jackson Brown, Jr. doesn't agree, he advises, "Never forget the three powerful resources you always have available to you: love, prayer and forgiveness."

Power means the capacity to exert an influence and the ability to act effectively. Make note of the times you influence or act effectively . . . you may be surprised.

Sharing Love

We are all familiar with romantic, passionate love. In case you have forgotten, research scientist Elaine Hatfield can refresh your memory. "Passionate lovers," explains Hatfield, "experience a roller coaster of feelings: euphoria, happiness, calm, tranquility, vulnerability, anxiety, panic, despair" (*Psychology Today*, March–April 1993). Love comes in many wrappers, some are plain and brown. There is also the warm and cozy "hot chocolate and bubble bath" love you share with your children, parents, siblings, pets, and friends. The simple act of giving love enhances your power. You have unlimited reservoirs of love. They will never run dry. When your love is returned something wonderful happens, your confidence and sense of well-being soar.

Yes, there is darker side, it is excruciating painful when a beloved mate does not return our gift of love. I have found that loving many people helps to cushion the painful emotional blow. We will still be sad, when we lose someone we value sadness is a given. However, our cherished supporters can envelop us in the warming comfort of their arms until we feel strong enough to sing "I Will Survive." It is risky to open your heart, to become vulnerable, and offer your precious love to a mate. I believe it is a risk worth taking. If he is worthy of you the relationship has the potential to become immeasurably fulfilling. If he is not worthy of you, you have choices to make.

Healthy loving will enhance your emotional strength and psychological well being. If you acknowledge and accept the possibility of loss and can honestly say to yourself "I would survive it" you have the power to give wholeheartedly. In contrast, fear of loss persistently whispers to "accept the unacceptable."

Wellness

A well body copes with stress more effectively and has fewer limitations. If you eat healthful foods, are physically active and take time for relaxation you will notice a positive impact on your psychological and emotional health.

External Power

If you attribute your power to an external source, such as other people or circumstances, you will frequently feel out of control or helpless. If you believe your future is determined by luck, fate or other outside influences, you believe in an external locus of control. If you believe you are the master of your fate and your decisions and efforts (within limits) will determine your future, then you believe in an internal locus of control. As we said earlier, many things, such as other people, are beyond your control. However, you have a great deal of power over your life.

The people who may seem wounded and helpless to you may have resources of which you are unaware. When they are helpless they are saying to you "I have no internal power." They are also saying "Someone must help me." There are times when we need help. However, when we are capable of successful effort we deserve the opportunity to succeed or fail on our own. Success builds self-confidence (if we assume credit for it) and a firm belief in our internal power to navigate life. Failure teaches us to look for other ways to solve a problem. The concepts of internal and external power (control) are equally important. At times fate will assume the reins. At those times look for something over which you have control and focus on that. When you can assume credit, give yourself a huge pat on the back. Accomplishing goals will strengthen your belief in yourself.

Ask yourself, what can I do to make my life better? Is my current intimate relationship in my best interest? What are my resources (i.e., support system, education, drive, intelligence) to make changes? What is my plan for making changes? How can I stop using manipulation in my life and relationships?

Mutual Manipulation

Couples frequently use manipulation as a tool to gain control. It isn't an effective tool, because the partners will not be happy or connected. Manipulation requires distance because it is an unfair and wounding tactic. Manipulation is shrouded in secrecy; by its very nature it must be to work. It one partner (or both) is taking unfair advantage of the other, intimacy will be discouraged. Manipulation is the couples' equivalent of cheating at cards. It will be noticed, if not directly, at least by a "discomfort" that says something is wrong.

As you learn more about Eric and Cynthia you will appreciate the insidious nature of manipulation.

A Tooth for a Tooth and an Eye for an Eye

Cynthia and Eric have been married for one year. Problems began almost immediately. Cynthia's physician referred them to me for couple's counseling.

They met at the suburban middle school where they are employed. This is the first marriage for Cynthia and the second for Eric. Eric is a thirty-five year old coach and Social Studies teacher. Cynthia is a twenty-nine year old Literature teacher. This was Cynthia's first job straight out of college. Eric has held a number of teaching positions. He says, "I can't remember the exact number of positions I have held. What difference does it make? That isn't why we are here." He is a large man with a ruddy complexion and red hair. Eric is dressed casually in tan slacks and an Oxford button-down shirt. He sits up straight on the sofa, leaning slightly forward toward me, as he glares at me.

Cynthia is tall and thin with short brown hair. She is slumped in a chair with her arms crossed over her chest and legs crossed at the ankles. Her legs are tucked under her chair. She is dressed rather matronly in a shapeless, drab brown dress and color coordinated sweater. Cynthia is wearing very little makeup and seems to be trying to reduce her size. Perhaps so we won't notice her? I ask her why they decided to begin counseling and why now? When she replies her voice is very soft and I have to lean forward more and listen intently. Eric says, "Why don't you speak up . . . don't be such a mouse." Cynthia begins again, "We argue all the time (she looks at Eric out of the corner of her eye, then down). I have a very delicate system and I cannot endure the stress. My health will break down completely soon. Eric is so robust he doesn't understand." I look at Eric. "She is always sick. You wouldn't believe our medical bills. She is breaking us with her illnesses." Cynthia, looking distinctly ill, comments, "I can't help being sick, Eric. You know how delicate I am. I really try to be stronger."

I take charge of the session again, "So tell me, what is the one issue, if resolved, that would make the most positive difference in your relationship?" Eric jumps in, "She doesn't do anything. She won't even have sex with me . . . other woman sure look at me. She is always too tired or sick." Cynthia looks aggrieved. She says, "You know that I do the very best I can with my limitations. You are always yelling at me." Cynthia looks at Eric and down again. She is putting more effort into disappearing.

Let's stop for a moment and determine what is happening between Eric and Cynthia. I notice that they are both using manipulative techniques. Cynthia is being passive-aggressive. I have spoken to her physician (with her written permission) and he tells me she is a healthy woman who will probably outlive all of us. Eric is using intimidation just as he does on the football field. He thinks he can bluster and yell and control her. So far, it isn't working. She is countering with "I can't help it, I am sick." He certainly cannot prove that she is well. Therefore, their marriage has become a vicious cycle for control. He yells. She plays sick to annoy him. He yells louder. She gets sicker. There are other issues, but the mutual manipulation is extremely destructive.

As I suspected, Cynthia grew up in a home with an authoritarian father and a timid mother. She says she was never close to her father because he was so intimidating. He would punish her severely for minor infractions. As protection she learned to become invisible. She was frequently sick with various mysterious sicknesses. They were not wealthy people and her medical bills were a burden. He had to work extra hours to made ends meet. Secretly, though she never admitted it to herself, she was glad he had to work overtime. She did not dare confront him, but she got her revenge. She is till getting her revenge, now with Eric.

Cynthia and I discussed her illnesses and their purpose. It would take awhile for Cynthia to learn to be direct and honest, to say, "I am angry with you." Eric decided he didn't need therapy, so Cynthia stayed to work on her self-confidence. After six months Cynthia regained and happily accepted her wellness. We used assertiveness training to help her be more assertive in many areas of her life. Independently, Eric worked on his caustic tendency to intimidate instead of negotiate. Cynthia kept a journal of her passive-aggressive and passive behaviors. We looked at her journal during each session and discussed more assertive approaches to replace her manipulative behaviors. We also worked on her negative beliefs about herself. She had many positive traits and strengths. She learned to acknowledge her personal power and achievements. Gradually, as she gained confidence, she began to stand up for herself, not just with Eric, she also went toe to toe with her dad. I wish you could have seen her face when she told me.

Eric and Cynthia continue to improve the way in which they interact with each other and the world. I am confident that they will continue to grow as a couple.

Conclusion

Know the difference between what you can control and what you cannot. Eric and Cynthia learned that they could not manipulate each other without negative consequences. Ask yourself, "Is this situation my responsibility?" before you jump in. Accept and appreciate yourself as you are at this moment. Decide in what areas you wish to grow. Use your power to make your world a better place. Your "better world" may or may not include your mate. You will recognize manipulative behaviors in your mate and/or in yourself. You can make healthy choices.

Dennis Waitley gives us something to ponder, "There are two primary *choices* in life: to accept conditions as they exist, or accept the responsibility for changing them." It is just that simple. You have the *power* to ask for what you need and desire. However, be prepared to accept the word "no." You have the *right* to expect and receive straightforward, honest communication from your mate.

References

Articles were retrieved from the Questia database (*www.questia.com*).

Bed and Broad. 1992. *National Review* 44 (February 17): 14+.

Bedard, P. 1998. Clinton Denies "Improper" Act with Willey. *Washington Times*, March 17, p. 1.

Beggan, J. K., and Allison, S. T. 2001. The Playboy Rabbit Is Soft, Furry, and Cute: Is This Really the Symbol of Masculine Dominance of Women? *Journal of Men's Studies* 9(3): 341.

Bornstein, R. F. 1998. Implicit and Self-Attributed Dependency Needs in Dependent and Histrionic Personality Disorders. *Journal of Personality Assessment* 71(1): 1–14.

Buss, D. M. 1995. Evolutionary Psychology: a New Paradigm for Psychological Science. *Psychological Inquiry* 6(1): 1–30.

———. 1998. Sexual Strategies Theory: Historical Origins and Current Status. *Journal of Sex Research* 35(1): 19+.

Cann, A., Mangum, J. L., and Wells, M. 2001. Distress in Response to Relationship Infidelity: The Roles of Gender and Attitudes about Relationships. *Journal of Sex Research* 38(3): 185+.

Cataldi, A. E., and Reardon, R. 1996. Gender, Interpersonal Orientation and Manipulation Tactic Use in Close Relationships. *Sex Roles: A Journal of Research* 35(3–4): 205+.

Collins, L. 1999. Emotional Adultery: Cybersex and Commitment. *Social Theory and Practice* 25(2): 243.

Cramer, R. E., and Manning-Ryan, B. 2000. Sex Differences in Subjective Distress to Violations of Trust: Extending an Evolutionary Perspective. *Basic and Applied Social Psychology* 22(2): 101–109.

Effects of Brief Training in Cooperation and Problem Solving on Success in Conflict Resolution. 1999. *Peace and Conflict* 5(2): 137–148.

Fields, S. 1998. Choosing Winners over Whiners. *Washington Times* (March 9), p. 15.

Griffin-Shelley, E. 1997. *Sex and Love Addiction, Treatment, and Recovery*. Westport, CT: Praeger.

Heatherton, T. F., and Weinberger, J. L., eds. 1994. *Can Personality Change?* Washington, DC: American Psychological Association.

Hughes, Z. 2003. Sisters, Beware! How to Spot a 'Playa'. *Ebony* 58(September): 100+.

Hughes, Z. 2000. Why Some Good Girls Prefer Bad Guys. *Ebony* 55(April): 84.

Irvine, J. M. 1995. Reinventing Perversion: Sex Addiction and Cultural Anxieties. *Journal of the History of Sexuality* 5(3): 429–450.

Jacobsberg, L., Perry, S., and Frances, A. 1995. Diagnostic Agreement Between the SCID-II Screening Questionnaire and the Personality Disorder Examination. *Journal of Personality Assessment* 65(3): 428–433.

Joiner, T. E., Metalsky, G. I., Katz, J., and Beach, S. R. 1999. Be (Re)Assured: Excessive Reassurance-Seeking Has (At Least) Some Explanatory Power Regarding Depression. *Psychological Inquiry* 10(4): 305–308.

Kang, M. 1997. The Portrayal of Women's Images in Magazine Advertisements: Goffman's Gender Analysis Revisited. *Sex Roles: A Journal of Research* 37(11–12): 979+.

Keen, S., and Zur, O. 1989. Who Is the Ideal Man? A Psychology Today Survey Report. *Psychology Today* 23(November): 54+. Retrieved July 11, 2005, from Questia database.

Kellerman, B. 1998. The Enabler. *Presidential Studies Quarterly* 28(4): 887.

Kisatsky, D. 1999. The Dark Side of Camelot. *Presidential Studies Quarterly* 29(1): 208.

Kramer, R. M. 1998. Paranoid Cognition in Social Systems: Thinking and Acting in the Shadow of Doubt. *Personality and Social Psychology Review,* 2(4): 251–275.

The Last Seduction. 1998. *National Review* (October 26): 42.

Lawson, W. 2004. Stolen Kisses: You Don't Want to Know How One in Five Couples Really Meet. *Psychology Today* 37(May/June): 13+.

Lazarus, A. A. 1994. Special Section. *Ethics & Behavior,* 4(3), 253–261.

Lowman, R. L. 1993. *Counseling and Psychotherapy of Work Dysfunctions.* Washington, DC: APA Books.

Martens, W. H. 2004. Optimal Involvement of Antisocial Patients in the Planning of Their Treatment Route: Some Positive Effects. *Annals of the American Psychotherapy Association* 7(4): 12+.

Mckay, G. 2000. The Myth of Monogamy: Fidelity and Infidelity in Animals and People. *Canadian Journal of Human Sexuality* 9(4): 275+.

Milhausen, R. R., and Herold, E. S. 1999. Does the Sexual Double Standard Still Exist? Perceptions of University Women. *Journal of Sex Research* 36(4): 361.

Murphy, J. 2005. Answering the Call Foster Family Opens Home, Hearts to Kids Who Need Care. *Daily Herald (Arlington Heights, IL)*, p. 1.

Norment, L. 1998. INFIDELITY II Why Women Cheat. *Ebony* (December): 148.

Pittman, F. 1993. Beyond Betrayal: Life after Infidelity. *Psychology Today* 26(May/June): 32+.

Randall, H. E., and Byers, E. S. 2003. What Is Sex? Students' Definitions of Having Sex, Sexual Partner and Unfaithful Sexual Behaviour. *Canadian Journal of Human Sexuality* 12(2): 87+.

Remember God's Blessings to Avoid the Whiners Club. 1996. *Washington Times*, October 21, p. 2.

Rodgers, J. E. 1999. FLIRTING Fascination. *Psychology Today* 32(January): 36.

Schlinger, H., and Barber, N. 2004. The Science of Romance: Secrets of the Sexual Brain. *Psychological Record* 54(1): 163+.

Spitzberg, B. H., and Cupach, W. R., eds. 1998. *The Dark Side of Close Relationships*. Mahwah, NJ: Lawrence Erlbaum Associates.

Sullivan, A. 1998. Sex, Lies and Us. *The Advocate*, October 27, pp. 53+.

Teachout, T. 2003. Mr. Personality. *Book*, July/August, p. 74.

They'll Take Manhattan. 2005. *American Theatre* 22(January): 22+.

Townsend, J. M. 1998. *What Women Want—What Men Want: Why the Sexes Still See Love and Commitment So Differently*. Oxford: Oxford University Press.

Wiederman, M. W. 1997. Extramarital Sex: Prevalence and Correlates in a National Survey. *Journal of Sex Research* 34(2): 167+.

Witham, L. 1998. Adultery No Moral Absolute in America. *Washington Times*, January 28, p. 1.

Index

About the Author

DR. DOROTHY MCCOY is a behavior expert, writer, and adjunct instructor at the South Carolina Criminal Justice Academy and a police consultant. She has spoken at international conferences on stress, panic attacks, police stress, and perception. Her behavior-change work has included stress management, anger management, weight loss, couple's issues, and reversing type II diabetes. Dr. McCoy has written more than sixty personality tests and various articles on personality. She has been in private practice for fifteen years and has tested hundreds of individuals.

Her other books include:

From Shyness to Social Butterfly, 2002

The Ultimate Book of Personality Tests, 2005

Reversing Type II Diabetes: A Step by Step Plan for Reclaiming Your Health, 2005